HEADS UP
PHILOSOPHY

**LONDON, NEW YORK,
MELBOURNE, MUNICH, AND DELHI**

Senior Project Editor Victoria Pyke
Project Editor Carron Brown
Editorial Assistant Ciara Ní Éanacháin
US Editors John Searcy, Allison Singer
Senior Designer Jim Green
Designers Daniela Boraschi, Mik Gates
Illustration Daniela Boraschi, Mik Gates,
Jim Green, Charis Tsevis

Managing Editor Linda Esposito
Managing Art Editor Michael Duffy
Publisher Andrew Macintyre
Publishing Director Jonathan Metcalf
Associate Publishing Director Liz Wheeler
Art Director Phil Ormerod
Pre-Production Producer Nikoleta Parasaki
Senior Producer Gemma Sharpe
Jacket Editor Maud Whatley
Jacket Designer Mark Cavanagh

Philosophers' biographies written by Clive Gifford
Introduction (pages 6–7) written by Stephen Law

First American Edition, 2014
Published in the United States by
DK Publishing
345 Hudson Street
New York, New York 10014

Copyright © 2014 Dorling Kindersley Limited
All rights reserved
14 15 16 17 18 10 9 8 7 6 5 4 3 2 1
001–192631–10/14

A catalog record for this book is available from the Library of Congress.

ISBN 978-1-4654-2448-8

Color reproduction by Altaimage, London
Printed and bound in Hong Kong

**Discover more at
www.dk.com**

HEADS UP
PHILOSOPHY

WRITTEN BY
MARCUS WEEKS

CONSULTANT
STEPHEN LAW

Contents

What is KNOWLEDGE?

What is REALITY?

What is the MIND?

What is REASONING?

What is RIGHT
and WRONG?

What is **PHILOSOPHY?**

WHY IS THERE ANYTHING AT ALL? WHAT MAKES THINGS RIGHT AND WRONG? DOES GOD EXIST? IN TRYING TO UNDERSTAND THE FUNDAMENTAL NATURE OF KNOWLEDGE, REALITY, AND EXISTENCE, PHILOSOPHY TACKLES SOME OF THE GREATEST MYSTERIES OF ALL. MANY SUCH QUESTIONS HAVE PUZZLED PHILOSOPHERS FOR CENTURIES. PHILOSOPHY DEVELOPED TO QUESTION WHAT PEOPLE OFTEN TAKE FOR GRANTED.

Many philosophical questions appear to be beyond the scope of science. Take moral questions, for instance. It's true that scientists can make morally significant discoveries. They can build nuclear weapons, or make it possible for us to design a baby by choosing his or her eye and hair color, and so on. But science cannot tell us whether we ought or ought not to use such new technologies. Science, it seems, is ultimately restricted to telling us how things are, whereas moral philosophy is concerned with how things *ought* to be. Doing philosophy involves trying to figure out as best we can what is true by using our powers of reason, or logical thought. It is an activity: a great way to learn how to think well—about anything. And the skills you pick up doing philosophy are skills you will find useful in all kinds of areas, from giving

a presentation to negotiating an important business deal. Philosophers also question our beliefs. We might not realize it, but we all hold a great many philosophical beliefs. These, of course, include moral beliefs: Many believe the universe was created by God, and that there is some form of life after death. Others believe the opposite. Often, we acquire our beliefs from our cultures, communities, and traditions. But these beliefs can change. Not so long ago, most Westerners thought it was morally acceptable to own slaves, and to prevent women from voting. Now, we know better. It is the role of the philosopher to try to establish whether or not such beliefs are true. In doing so, philosophers may be considered an annoyance. But it is important that we ask these questions. After all, the answers really do matter.

What do
PHILOSOPHERS DO?

HOW CAN I LEARN ABOUT PHILOSOPHY?

Many schools, colleges, and universities offer courses in philosophy, leading to formal degrees. Philosophy is sometimes taught as a part of courses in other subjects, such as politics, economics, theology, and psychology.

Academic courses

There is a growing interest in philosophy as a hobby, and philosophy groups have become popular, allowing like-minded people to meet and discuss philosophy in an informal setting. Evening classes are also available in many areas.

Discussion groups

WHAT SKILLS CAN PHILOSOPHY GIVE ME?

Philosophy is all about reasoning—rational thought. Learning about philosophy, and discussing philosophical problems with others, is good exercise for the mind, and teaches us the skills of clear and logical thinking.

Clear thinking

Philosophical debate is a good way to develop the skills of presenting an argument. In addition to providing good reasons for an opinion, a convincing argument has to be presented logically, using unambiguous language.

Presentation skills

WHAT CAREER PATHS DO PHILOSOPHERS FOLLOW?

The skills of argument and a knowledge of moral philosophy are very useful in the legal profession. Many philosophers have become lawyers and judges, as well as mediators, and they also advise on ethics in science, medicine, and business.

Law

Some philosophers have taken up careers as politicians, political advisers, or activists. Many also work in the civil service, advising the government on economic, social, and international policy, and how it can be implemented.

Public policy

VERY FEW PEOPLE EARN THEIR LIVING AS FULL-TIME PHILOSOPHERS, EITHER WRITING PHILOSOPHICAL BOOKS OR TEACHING AND RESEARCHING IN UNIVERSITIES. STUDYING PHILOSOPHY, HOWEVER, HELPS US DEVELOP SKILLS THAT ARE USEFUL IN MANY DIFFERENT JOBS, AND PHILOSOPHERS FOLLOW A WIDE VARIETY OF CAREER PATHS. ALSO, A LOT OF PEOPLE SIMPLY ENJOY PHILOSOPHY FOR ITS OWN SAKE, AS A HOBBY.

There are some philosophy magazines aimed at the general reader—these are usually available by subscription rather than at bookstores. They may also be available online, along with a number of blogs about philosophy.

Magazines and blogs

No matter how you choose to learn about philosophy, you'll want to browse your library or bookstore for books by philosophers. There are also several encyclopedias and dictionaries of philosophy, and many of the best are available online.

Books

One of the core skills of philosophy is being able to recognize the strengths and weaknesses of an argument. Often, this involves seeing things from both sides, and finding the middle ground between two opposing views.

Negotiating and mediating

Logic in particular teaches us practical thinking skills, techniques that help us make rational decisions. These are useful in approaching tasks in a systematic, methodical way, and organizing and planning solutions to problems.

Problem solving

Above all, philosophy teaches us not simply to accept conventional wisdom. Philosophers demand rational justification rather than faith or prejudice, and can offer new ideas as well as challenge beliefs.

Independent thinking

Reporters, investigative journalists, political commentators, and editors need to be able to get to the heart of a story quickly and present it clearly through the media. Philosophy provides many of the skills required for a career in journalism.

Journalism

While some philosophers have chosen to become entrepreneurs, many more have found that philosophy has provided them with skills that can be applied to marketing and advertising, or to business organization and human resources.

Business

The philosophy of mind has obvious connections with psychology, and many psychologists and neuroscientists have studied philosophy. Some philosophy students have also trained to become psychotherapists and counselors.

Mental health

In addition to professional philosophers, who generally work in universities and colleges, there are many students of philosophy working in education, as teachers of a variety of subjects, but also as educational theorists.

Education

What is KNOWLEDGE?

The NEED to KNOW

How do you KNOW that?

Where did you get that IDEA?

Don't trust your SENSES

Knowledge comes from REASONING

We learn from EXPERIENCE

Take NOTHING for granted

BELIEVING is not the same as KNOWING

You can NEVER know it ALL

Do we ever really know the TRUTH?

Epistemology is the branch of philosophy concerned with knowledge: what knowledge is, and how we acquire it. One of the major areas of debate is how much we can acquire knowledge of things from our experience of the world, and how much we can know through reasoning—and also if there are limits to what we can ever know.

The NEED to KNOW

IT IS HUMAN NATURE TO BE INQUISITIVE. WE HAVE A NEED TO UNDERSTAND THE WORLD AROUND US AND OUR PLACE IN IT, AS WELL AS THE WAY WE THINK AND BEHAVE. OUR SEARCH FOR KNOWLEDGE DEMANDS EXPLANATIONS— INCLUDING EXPLANATIONS OF HOW WE COME TO KNOW THINGS AND IF WE CAN BE SURE OF WHAT WE KNOW.

See also: 14–15, 16–17

Traditional beliefs

From the very earliest times, people have wondered about and tried to understand the world they live in. They looked for explanations, especially of the natural phenomena that affected their lives—for example, the changing seasons and when plants grow and die, the rising and setting of the sun and moon, and the movements of the stars. For prehistoric people, these were like a kind of magic, and were often explained as the work of supernatural forces. Religions and myths evolved that gave explanations not only of the physical world but also of the way we behave, according to laws given to us by the gods. And as civilizations became established, these traditional beliefs formed the basis of cultures, a framework for society, and were passed on from generation to generation almost unquestioningly. But as societies grew more sophisticated, some people found that tradition no longer satisfied their curiosity—rather than accepting conventional beliefs, they wanted to find their own answers.

Rational explanations

It was from this desire to know about the world, and not just believe what religion or tradition told them, that the first philosophers emerged in ancient Greece. They challenged accepted ideas and sought alternative answers to their questions by examining the world and using their ability to think, or reason. In doing so, they felt that their rational explanations would provide them with knowledge, rather than just belief.

REASON IS IMMORTAL, ALL ELSE MORTAL.

PYTHAGORAS

WE UNLOCK KNOWLEDGE IN DIFFERENT WAYS...

TRADITION

REASONING

◉ The missing key?

The earliest philosophers challenged traditional explanations of the world and how we live in it. They sought alternative explanations, and used reasoning to examine the world in a new way.

MANY THINGS PREVENT KNOWLEDGE, INCLUDING THE OBSCURITY OF THE SUBJECT AND THE BREVITY OF HUMAN LIFE.

PROTAGORAS

These early philosophers tried to find explanations for the makeup and structure of the world, a search that evolved into the various branches of science. Later philosophers, on the other hand, attempted to provide rational explanations of how we should live our lives, and the nature of reality and our existence, as alternatives to traditional beliefs. This way of examining and attempting to understand the world by reasoning, and especially by encouraging discussion and debate, is what philosophy is all about, and even today it often questions the conventions of the society we live in.

The problem of knowledge

While philosophy emerged from our human desire for knowledge, philosophers also turned their attention to knowledge itself. They began to feel that it was no longer enough simply to say "that's the way things are," or even to explain why we think that—we must also examine how we know that. By the time Greek civilization had peaked with the establishment of the city-state of Athens, philosophers had started to question what we mean when we say we know something, and what knowledge actually is. This was the birth of the branch of philosophy called epistemology, which is concerned with all aspects of knowledge: how we acquire knowledge, how we can be sure of what we know, and if there are some things that we can never know.

the word *philosophy* comes from a greek word that means "love of wisdom."

IN THE BEGINNING

While city-states were being established in ancient Greece, civil societies were also developing in China and India. These too produced original thinkers, including Kong Fuzi (Confucius) and Siddhartha Gautama (the Buddha), but they took a very different approach. In Eastern philosophy, the focus is mainly on questions of how we can live a good life and how to organize society, and the boundaries between philosophy and religion are less clear-cut than in Western philosophy.

How do you KNOW that?

WE OFTEN SAY THAT WE KNOW SOMETHING, WHEN IN FACT WE ARE SIMPLY ACCEPTING SOMEBODY ELSE'S OPINION OR A CONVENTIONAL EXPLANATION. FOR PHILOSOPHERS, IT IS NOT ENOUGH JUST TO ACCEPT THAT SOMETHING IS TRUE. THEY NEED TO HAVE A GOOD REASON FOR BELIEVING IT, BACKED UP BY A CONVINCING ARGUMENT.

> Socrates was both wise and honest—before he was sentenced to death, he paid off his last debt with a chicken.

Finding truths through reason

Not satisfied with conventional or religious explanations, early philosophers in ancient Greece used reasoning to try to understand the world. They formed new ideas about the makeup and structure of the world, and came up with reasoned arguments to back up their theories. From this emerged the notion that to

> **NO MAN KNOWS DISTINCTLY ANYTHING, AND NO MAN EVER WILL.**
> XENOPHANES

know something, rather than simply believe it to be true, requires the use of reason, and that, on this basis, reason is the source of all of our real knowledge. But not all ancient Greek philosophers supposed that they could answer all the big questions just by thinking. Xenophanes, for example, agreed that rational thinking is important, but argued that this needs to be backed up with evidence from the outside world to prevent it from being just speculation.

We know nothing

Gradually, the emphasis of philosophical discussion shifted from questions about the nature of the universe to the question of how we know things: not only how we can be sure of what we know, but also how we come to know things— where our knowledge comes from. At about the same time that Athens became the cultural center of ancient Greece in the 5th century BCE, philosophers became more interested in human concerns, such as morality and politics, and the problem of knowledge. Foremost among them was Socrates, who questioned conventional ideas and beliefs, using his ability to reason to establish what we do and don't really know. His method was to engage other people in discussion about the things they believed they knew, but in order to remove all preconceived ideas, he adopted the standpoint that he himself knew nothing. He then challenged all the ideas and assumptions of the person he was talking with, pointing out the contradictions and shortcomings of their arguments, and showing the limitations of their knowledge. What Socrates

FINISH · KNOWLEDGE · ? · ? · ? · ? · START · IGNOR

AS FOR ME, ALL I KNOW IS THAT I KNOW NOTHING.

SOCRATES

See also: 12–13, 20–21

THE WISEST OF ALL

The oracle at Delphi said that there was no one wiser than Socrates, yet Socrates always maintained he knew nothing—how could he be the wisest man? But when he discussed philosophy with the greatest men of Athens, he realized they only thought they knew a lot. He was wiser than all of them because he was aware of the limitations of his knowledge.

demonstrated most effectively, though, was the power of reason to expose the weakness of assumed knowledge, and how rational thought can provide an insight into a deeper knowledge of things.

Challenging knowledge

Socrates set out not just to challenge the accepted beliefs of the time, but, in doing that, to try to find truths that we can have knowledge of. He was particularly interested in issues of morality and politics, and asked questions such as "What is justice?" or "What is courage?" Although most people believed they knew the answers to these questions, he showed that they did not. Many of the people he debated with could provide examples of just or courageous actions as evidence to back up their beliefs, but could not identify what all of these things had in common. What Socrates was looking for in this kind of discussion was not a simple definition of what we mean by *justice* or *courage*, but the essence of what justice and courage really are. And he supposed that this essence was something we can only know through reasoning.

GAME OF KNOWLEDGE

THE PATH TO KNOWLEDGE IS PAVED WITH MANY QUESTIONS.

◐ Question everything
Socrates believed that we are born knowing nothing, but that we acquire knowledge as we go through life by questioning the beliefs and conventions we encounter at every stage.

Where did you get

ONE OF THE FUNDAMENTAL QUESTIONS OF EPISTEMOLOGY, THE BRANCH OF PHILOSOPHY CONCERNED WITH KNOWLEDGE, IS WHERE OUR KNOWLEDGE COMES FROM. EVER SINCE ANCIENT GREEK TIMES, PHILOSOPHERS HAVE ARGUED ABOUT WHETHER WE ARE BORN WITH KNOWLEDGE OF AT LEAST SOME THINGS, OR IF THAT KNOWLEDGE COMES FROM EXPERIENCE.

Two schools of thought

Theories of how we come to have knowledge of things have divided philosophers' opinions roughly into two different camps throughout much of the history of philosophy. Those in the first camp have argued that we are born with an ability to reason, and it is that innate ability that allows us to acquire knowledge. Rationalism, the view that reason is the main source of our knowledge, regards reality as consisting of truths, which we can discover by reasoning. Those in the second camp, on the other hand, have argued that we have no innate abilities or knowledge, and that our knowledge is learned from our experience of the world outside us. This view, known as empiricism, considers the information we gather through our senses to be the primary source of knowledge.

The word *epistemology* comes from two greek words, meaning "study of knowledge."

ARE WE BORN WITH KNOWLEDGE?

WHAT WE CALL LEARNING IS ONLY A PROCESS OF RECOLLECTION.

PLATO

Discovering innate knowledge

Among early philosophers in ancient Greece, the emphasis was on the power of reasoning. They believed that knowledge could be acquired through reason alone. Plato demonstrated this by telling the story of Socrates discussing a problem in geometry with a slave boy who had never learned geometry. By watching Socrates drawing diagrams in the sand, the boy understood how the problem could be solved by reasoning. Socrates had not told him the answer, but the boy knew he had discovered the solution. Plato argued that the boy had no experience of the problem or its solution, and concluded that it was knowledge he already had—innate knowledge—which he accessed by reasoning. We are born with knowledge of certain truths, he proposed, which exist in a "world

that **IDEA**?

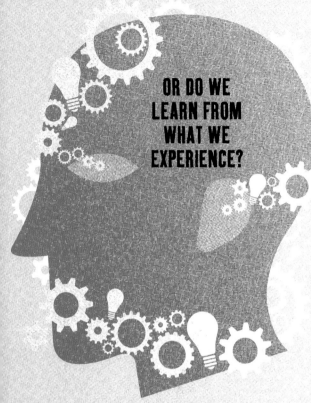

OR DO WE
LEARN FROM
WHAT WE
EXPERIENCE?

◉ Any idea?
Plato and the rationalists believed that we are born with knowledge, which we can retrieve through reasoning. But Aristotle and the empiricists argued that we acquire all our knowledge of the outside world through our senses.

believed that we are born knowing nothing, and that our knowledge is built on what we learn from our experience of the world. This empirical argument resurfaced after the medieval period, with the rise of scientific discoveries based on observation (or experience), rather than theorizing (reasoning about what we know). René Descartes returned to Plato's ideas in the 17th century, prompting a reaction from John Locke, who, like Aristotle, rejected the rationalist notion of innate knowledge. One of the foremost empiricist philosophers, Locke believed that knowledge of the world outside us comes from our experience of it, and the only direct interface between our minds and the outside world is our senses. We can use reason to rationalize the information from our senses and formulate ideas, but anything that does not originate from sensory experience has no link with external reality, and can give us no knowledge of it.

See also: 18–19, 20–21, 24–25

of ideas," separate from the world of the senses. These truths are the source of all our knowledge, rather than what we experience with our senses.

A link to reality
While Plato's ideas of knowledge were accepted by many philosophers for several centuries, one of his pupils offered a very different view. Aristotle did not accept that we have innate knowledge. Instead, he

ALL MEN BY NATURE DESIRE KNOWLEDGE.

ARISTOTLE

NEW IDEAS
Both Plato and Aristotle founded schools of philosophy, the Academy and the Lyceum, not to teach their particular point of view, but to inspire philosophical discussion. Although philosophers disagree about the original source of knowledge, it is almost universally accepted that it is through reasoning, and especially philosophical argument and debate, that new ideas emerge.

See also: 14–15, 16–17, 20–21, 24–25, 44–45

DO THINGS CEASE TO EXIST ONCE WE STOP LOOKING AT THEM?

Vanishing world ❯
Some philosophers believed that we can only gain knowledge through our senses. George Berkeley went so far as to doubt the existence of anything material—if we can't sense things behind us, how can we know they even exist?

Don't trust

WE TEND TO ACCEPT THAT OUR SENSES GIVE US A FAIRLY ACCURATE IDEA OF THE WORLD AROUND US—"SEEING IS BELIEVING". BUT WE ALSO KNOW THAT THEY CAN BE FOOLED—FOR EXAMPLE, BY OPTICAL ILLUSIONS. DOES THIS MAKE SENSES AN UNRELIABLE SOURCE OF KNOWLEDGE? IF THEY CAN BE DECEIVED, MAYBE WE CAN'T TRUST ANYTHING WE LEARN FROM THEM.

An imperfect world

One of the first philosophers to tackle the problem of how untrustworthy our senses are as a source of knowledge was Plato. Like his mentor, Socrates, he set out to show that many of the things that people take for granted—the things they think they know—are based on unreliable sources. He argued that not only do our senses often let us down, but also that the world we live in and experience with our senses is imperfect.

george berkeley peaked early—he wrote all of his best-known works while he was still in his twenties.

For example, when we see a circle drawn on a piece of paper, we recognize it as a circle. But it is not a perfect circle—no matter how carefully it is drawn or printed, a perfect circle cannot exist in the world we live in. Nothing, Plato said, exists in its perfect, ideal form in our world. It is an illusory world, made up of imperfect versions of things, and what we learn about it through our senses must also be imperfect knowledge.

Our senses can be tricked

The idea that our senses may be deceiving us was later taken up by the French philosopher and mathematician René Descartes. He realized that sometimes our senses give us a false impression—a straight stick in a glass of water appears to be bent, for example. And if we know

EVERYTHING THAT DECEIVES MAY BE SAID TO ENCHANT.

PLATO

your SENSES

> ## THE SENSES DECEIVE FROM TIME TO TIME, AND IT IS PRUDENT NEVER TO TRUST WHOLLY THOSE WHO HAVE DECEIVED US EVEN ONCE.
>
> ### RENÉ DESCARTES

that they can be unreliable, it would be wrong to trust them completely—everything that we experience with our senses might be false. It might even be that we are asleep, and that the world we are experiencing is no more than a dream, or that God or some mischievous power is making us believe things that are not really true. If that is the case, though, we can never know anything for sure. But Descartes then showed that there was one thing he could be sure of: In order to be deceived, he must exist, and exist as a thing that thinks. So, although his senses could not be trusted, he could be sure he existed as something that was capable of thinking and reasoning.

Only the things we experience exist

Although many 17th-century philosophers accepted Descartes's argument, not everybody agreed. Some, especially in Britain, accepted that our senses can be unreliable, but believed that they are the only source of our knowledge. We have a power of reasoning, but

this does not provide us with knowledge—it is what we use to make sense of the information coming to us from our senses. We can only know about things that we experience, and we can only experience these things through our senses. This view, empiricism, was taken to an extreme by Bishop George Berkeley. We get our knowledge from our experience of things, but, he suggested, all we can ever experience is the ideas of those things in our minds. We don't have any real grounds for believing that anything exists other than those ideas. The only things whose existence we can be sure of are ideas and the minds that perceive them—according to Berkeley, nothing material exists.

THE DECEIVING DEMON

René Descartes wanted to imagine a situation in which it would be absolutely impossible to trust anything his senses were telling him. To do this, he devised a thought experiment— an imaginary situation— in which an evil demon had the power to deceive him and make him believe something, even though it was not true.

Knowledge comes

ALTHOUGH IT SEEMS AS THOUGH WE
FIND OUT ABOUT THE WORLD FROM
WHAT WE SEE, HEAR, TOUCH, TASTE,
AND SMELL, OUR SENSES ARE NOT
PERFECT, AND THEY GIVE US AN
IMPERFECT IDEA OF REALITY. BUT WE
HAVE ANOTHER FACULTY, OUR ABILITY
TO USE RATIONAL THOUGHT, WHICH
MANY PHILOSOPHERS SEE AS A MORE
RELIABLE SOURCE OF KNOWLEDGE.

> plato argued
> that men and women
> have the same intellectual
> powers and should receive
> the same education.

All objects have an ideal form

The idea that what we experience of
the world is deceptive is central to
the philosophy of Plato. He argued
that our senses merely give us an
impression of reality, and that it is only
by reasoning, or thinking logically, that we
can gain knowledge of the true nature of
things. His mentor, Socrates, had asked
questions such as "What is justice?" and
"What is virtue?" to try to find their nature
or essence. Rather than simply point out
instances that exemplified justice or
virtue, Socrates thought that an ideal form
of these things must exist. Plato took this
idea further. He believed that there are
not only ideal forms of abstract things
such as justice and virtue, but that there
are ideal forms of objects too, and what
we experience with our senses are just
imperfect reflections of those forms.
For example, when we see a chair,
we recognize it as a chair even though
there are all kinds of different chairs in
the world. He argued that this is because
we have an idea in our minds of an ideal
chair, and the chair we see is an example—
an imperfect "copy"—of that ideal form.

The world of ideas

Plato explained that these perfect forms
of things actually exist, but in a world
separate from the world we live in. Our
world contains only imperfect shadows of
the ideal forms. But although this world
of ideas (or forms, as he called them) is
outside of space and time, we can have
access to it because we are born with a
knowledge of those perfect ideas. We can,
for instance, recognize a triangle, even
though its sides may not be perfectly
straight, because we have an innate idea
in our minds of what a perfect triangle

EARTHLY KNOWLEDGE IS BUT SHADOW.

PLATO

from **REASONING**

REASONING SHAPES OUR KNOWLEDGE.

⊙ Perfect shadows
Plato believed that although we can identify circles and squares, for example, these are imperfect reflections of perfect forms. Perfect circles and squares do not exist in the world we live in.

looks like. Furthermore, by reasoning, we can work out that the three angles of that triangle add up to 180°, a straight line, and know that it is true. Plato considered our everyday world to be illusory (not real), and thought that true reality exists only in the world of ideas. And while our senses give us an imperfect picture of a world of shadows, true knowledge of reality can only be acquired through reasoning.

Two plus two always equals four
Plato's notion that rational thought is the chief source of our knowledge was also at the heart of the philosophical approach started by René Descartes in the 17th century. Descartes took the view that, because our senses can be deceived, the only things we can truly know are those we have learned from reasoning. As an accomplished mathematician, he recognized that mathematical truths, especially in geometry, can be discovered purely using rational thought—by working in logical steps from one truth to another to reach a conclusion. He also believed

that everything in the universe has a logical structure, which can be discovered in the same way. Rationalism, as this view came to be known, appealed especially to mathematicians, including Benedictus Spinoza and Gottfried Leibniz, who followed in Descartes's footsteps. In the 17th and 18th centuries, a period of great advances in mathematics, rationalism became the dominant approach to philosophy in Europe.

See also: 14–15, 18–19

PLATO'S CAVE
To explain his theory of the world of ideas, Plato told the story of prisoners held in a cave with their backs to the entrance. Behind them is a fire, which casts shadows of objects onto the back wall of the cave. For the prisoners, these shadows are the only reality they understand, unless they can free themselves to turn around and realize they are only the shadows of real objects.

DAVID HUME

1711–1776

Scottish philosopher David Hume was only 12 when he enrolled at Edinburgh University. He studied law, but preferred philosophy. After working as a clerk in Bristol, England, and studying at La Flèche, the French college that René Descartes had attended a century earlier, Hume refined and communicated his philosophy with modest success. Only after his death did his true worth become clear.

YOUNG AUTHOR

Living a frugal life, Hume completed *A Treatise of Human Nature* while in his twenties. It was published in 1739–1740 to a handful of lukewarm reviews, even though it was to become a hugely important work. Undeterred, Hume published volumes of essays and simplified his earlier work to create well-received publications such as *An Enquiry Concerning Human Understanding* (1748).

After he wasn't allowed to order certain books for the library where he worked, Hume gave his salary in protest to blind poet Thomas Blacklock.

EMPIRICISM AND UTILITY

Hume was an empiricist who believed that significant knowledge of reality could be obtained only through the senses. These perceptions, however, were individual and not universal. He also proposed that human passions, not reason, governed behavior, and that moral principles were not based on God's will but on their utility or usefulness to people.

THE BEST-SELLING HISTORIAN

Hume failed to obtain posts at universities in Glasgow and Edinburgh, so he worked as a librarian at the Edinburgh Faculty of Advocates from 1752. With access to the library's 30,000 books, Hume researched and wrote the monumental six-volume *History of England* (1754). Containing more than a million words, it proved to be an unlikely best seller, being reprinted at least 100 times.

"**Reason** is... the **slave of the passions**, and can never pretend to any other office than to **serve** and **obey** them."

RELEGATING RELIGION

As a child, Hume attended church, but as an adult he angered many by arguing that knowledge is not received from God but results from experiences. He criticized the foundations on which some religions were based, and in *A Treatise of Human Nature* wrote: "Generally speaking, the errors in religion are dangerous; those in philosophy only ridiculous."

We learn from EXPERIENCE

WHILE MANY PHILOSOPHERS THROUGHOUT HISTORY HAVE THOUGHT THAT REASONING IS THE MAIN SOURCE OF OUR KNOWLEDGE, OTHERS HAVE ARGUED THAT WHAT WE KNOW ABOUT THE WORLD COMES CHIEFLY FROM EXPERIENCE. WE ARE BORN KNOWING NOTHING, AND ACQUIRE KNOWLEDGE THROUGH THE USE OF OUR SENSES.

> **TRUTH RESIDES IN THE WORLD AROUND US.**
> ARISTOTLE

A blank slate

From its beginnings in ancient Greece, philosophy relied upon rational thought to provide answers and explanations. Reasoning was considered so important—more important than experience through our imperfect senses—that Plato thought that all our knowledge comes from reason. Other philosophers, however, disagreed, and felt that our experience of the world is also important in establishing truth and acquiring knowledge. And Aristotle took almost totally the opposite view from Plato. When we are born, he said, our minds are like a slate with nothing written on it, and we build up our knowledge of the world we live in from our experience of it—what we see, hear, touch, taste, and smell.

The essence of things

Aristotle argued that the things we experience in the world we live in are not, as Plato thought, imperfect versions of ideal forms existing in a separate world. Rather than having an innate idea of the perfect form of something, and then recognizing imperfect examples of it, we build up an idea of what makes it what it is from our experience of various instances of that thing. For example, from seeing many dogs, we learn various things all dogs have in common. These things make up what Aristotle calls the "form" of a dog, its essence, which does not exist in a separate world, but is present in each instance of a dog. It is our experience of particular instances of things that gives us knowledge of their essential nature—not just objects in the natural world, but also concepts such as justice and virtue. At birth, we have no innate ideas of right and wrong, for example, but we learn to recognize the qualities that instances of them have in common and build an understanding of what they essentially are.

With experience comes knowledge

Aristotle's notion that experience is the main source of our knowledge influenced the growth of science, especially at the end of the Middle Ages when major scientific discoveries were made through observation

> **LET US SUPPOSE THE MIND TO BE WHITE PAPER, VOID OF ALL CHARACTERS, WITHOUT ANY IDEAS; HOW COMES IT TO BE FURNISHED?**
> JOHN LOCKE

WE BUILD UP AN IDEA OF A DOG FROM ALL THE DIFFERENT DOGS WE HAVE SEEN.

Aristotle liked to walk and talk—in order to learn, his students had to follow him.

and experimentation. While rationalist philosophers such as René Descartes were inspired by the abstract reasoning of mathematics, others attributed the growth of knowledge in the natural sciences to experience. This view, known as empiricism, was popular among British philosophers such as John Locke. Like Aristotle, he believed that we are born with no knowledge, and that everything we know comes from the information gathered by our senses. We gradually organize that information to form a general view of the world, by associating things to form complex ideas, and developing our ability to apply reason to what we experience.

⊙ Piecing it together

From our experience of many dogs, we can recognize the characteristics that give them their "dogginess," such as fur or a tail. This "form" is common to all dogs, and helps us identify a dog even when it is only partly visible.

NATURE LOVER

Aristotle was a keen naturalist who made a detailed study of wildlife, classifying things into different groups of plants and animals. He organized these categories by identifying certain characteristics, such as whether an animal can fly or swim, and whether it has feathers, scales, or fur. He then grouped things together in "families," recognizable by their common characteristics.

See also: 18–19, 20–21

CERTAINTY

WE CAN'T KNOW ANYTHING FOR CERTAIN...

Take NOTHING

PHILOSOPHERS DO NOT SIMPLY ACCEPT STATEMENTS AS TRUE, BUT CHALLENGE WHETHER OR NOT THERE ARE GROUNDS FOR BELIEVING THAT THEY ARE TRUE. DOUBT IS A USEFUL TOOL IN PHILOSOPHY, HELPING TO ESTABLISH WHAT IS CERTAIN, AND WHAT IS NOT. BUT IS THERE ANYTHING ABOUT WHICH WE CAN BE CERTAIN?

DOUBT IS THE ORIGIN OF WISDOM.

RENÉ DESCARTES

What can we be certain of?

Philosophers since the time of Socrates have debated whether we can be certain of what we know, or even if we can know anything at all. Socrates himself took the view that it was possible to have knowledge, but in order to reach this conclusion he had to start from the standpoint that he knew nothing. He then tried to gain knowledge by discussing issues with people. By questioning everything that they thought they knew, he was able to point out the inconsistencies and contradictions in their beliefs. A later group of Greek philosophers, the skeptics,

socrates's wife, xanthippe, is said to have been the only person who ever defeated him in an argument.

supposed that we cannot be certain of, or know about, anything. But not all philosophers have taken such an extreme view. Some have taken a skeptical stance to help them establish what we can know for sure. They use doubt as a tool—applying it to all beliefs to discover which are certain. Although some skeptics still maintain that absolute knowledge of anything is impossible, others believe that it is possible to know some things, but not others. And a degree of skepticism is necessary for any philosophical enquiry, until you have a convincing argument or evidence that something is true beyond reasonable doubt.

I don't doubt that I exist

René Descartes took the approach of a skeptic in order to see if he could find a solid base for his philosophy—something that could not be doubted. He came up with an imaginary situation, a skeptical hypothesis, in which an evil demon was deceiving him to the extent that he

... SO SHOULD WE QUESTION EVERYTHING?

ARE YOU SURE?

for granted

doubted everything his senses told him. In doing so, he effectively took the standpoint of an out-and-out skeptic, doubting the truth of absolutely everything. But he realized that because he was able to doubt everything, he must exist in order to do the doubting. The fact of his existence was the first thing Descartes found that he could not doubt—it was an undoubtable truth, which he could use to build his arguments upon.

Use your common sense

A century later, Scottish philosopher David Hume also adopted a skeptical approach. As an empiricist, he thought that we acquire our knowledge through experience via our senses, but he also realized that these are not perfect, and may give us false information. In the same way, he recognized that logical reasoning was equally unreliable, and concluded that we can't know anything with absolute certainty. For example, he thought it was impossible to justify our belief that the sun will rise tomorrow, on the basis that it has always risen in the past. But he accepted that we cannot help but believe the sun will rise. Hume also reasoned that we should "proportion our beliefs to the evidence," believing when there is good

> IN OUR **REASONINGS** CONCERNING **FACT,** THERE ARE ALL **IMAGINABLE DEGREES** OF ASSURANCE. A **WISE MAN** THEREFORE PROPORTIONS HIS **BELIEF** TO THE **EVIDENCE.**
> **DAVID HUME**

evidence to support what we believe, and doubting when there is not. The evidence for miracles, for instance, is poor, and any claim that a miracle has occurred, contrary to the laws of nature, is unlikely to be true. The more likely explanation is that our senses are deceiving us, or the person telling us about the miracle is doing so.

See also: 14–15, 18–19

INFINITE REGRESS

If we question whether a statement is true or not, we are asking if there is a good argument for it. The trouble is, any argument supporting it will involve other statements—which a skeptic will say can also be doubted. And to back these up, we offer yet more statements, which can be doubted too. This never-ending process is known as infinite regress.

BELIEVING is not the same as KNOWING

WE THINK WE KNOW A LOT OF THINGS. BUT MAYBE IT ISN'T THAT SIMPLE—WE COULD MISTAKENLY BELIEVE SOMETHING THAT TURNS OUT NOT TO BE TRUE, OR ACCEPT AS FACT SOMETHING SOMEBODY HAS TOLD US, WITHOUT CHECKING WHETHER THERE'S ANY REASON TO BELIEVE IT. THE QUESTION IS, WHEN DO WE REALLY KNOW SOMETHING?

Belief or knowledge?

We often use the word *belief* when talking about religious faith: Members of a religion believe in a god or gods, and believe what is written in their holy scriptures. In philosophy, we investigate whether or not what we believe is really true. Philosophers acknowledge that we accept many things as true—and many of our beliefs may, in fact, be true. But that doesn't mean we know, however. People often claim that they "just know" something, and while they may be right, we instinctively feel that they don't actually know it because they cannot give a good reason for believing it. Other people do give

❯ Deceptive appearance
Driving down this road, you might be justified in believing that these houses are real because, from the front, they look real. But the houses are, in fact, fake, so this is not a true belief.

THE BELIEF THAT THESE HOUSES ARE REAL IS NOT KNOWLEDGE.

reasons for believing what they do, but their reasons are not very good. Again, it seems right to say that they don't really know.

Justified true belief

One of the first philosophers to try to examine exactly what distinguished knowing from believing was Plato, who defined knowledge as "justified true belief." To know something, we must believe it to be true, and we must have good reason for believing it is true, but it must also actually be true. For example, I might truly believe that Santa Claus exists, and I'm justified in believing it because I've seen the presents he

KNOWLEDGE IS JUSTIFIED TRUE BELIEF.
PLATO

leaves, but we can't say that I know he exists because, in reality, he doesn't—it isn't a true belief. Alternatively, I might genuinely believe that I'll win the lottery one day, which might, in fact, turn out to be true, but I have no justification for believing that, so again, I can't say that I know it. To be real knowledge, my belief must be both true and justified.

FAITH OR REASON?

Medieval Christian philosophers sometimes found a conflict when they attempted to use Greek philosophical arguments to justify their beliefs. In Eastern philosophy, however, religious beliefs, such as the cycle of birth and rebirth, were simply accepted as a matter of faith rather than philosophical debate.

The Gettier problem

Most philosophers accepted Plato's definition of knowledge as justified true belief until the 1960s, when Edmund Gettier showed that it didn't always provide a satisfactory explanation. He came up with several instances where we instinctively realize that someone doesn't really know something, even though that person's belief is both true and justified. For example, I have arranged to meet my friend Sue at her house, and when I arrive I see her through the window sitting in the kitchen. In fact, it is not Sue that I see, but her identical twin sister—Sue is actually in another room. My belief that Sue is home is true, and I have good reason to believe it because I am sure I have seen her, but it is wrong to say that I knew she was at home—I didn't know. Examples such as this became known as "Gettier problems," and have prompted philosophers to ask if, in addition to belief, truth, and justification, there is a fourth criterion for knowledge. Gettier had cast doubt not only on Plato's definition, but also on whether or not it is possible to define completely what knowledge is.

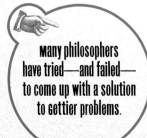

Many philosophers have tried—and failed—to come up with a solution to gettier problems.

IMMANUEL KANT

1724–1804

Immanuel Kant lived all his life in the Baltic Sea port of Königsberg (now Kaliningrad, Russia). He was a predictable fellow, and townsfolk set their clocks by the regularity of his daily walk. After almost a decade as a private tutor, he became an unsalaried lecturer at the University of Königsberg, paid only by the students who attended. He was later made a professor there.

THE IMPORTANCE OF THE MIND

In his *Critique of Pure Reason* (1781), Kant proposed that to find answers to philosophical problems, people had to examine their own minds, looking inward rather than examining the world around them. Philosophy, according to Kant, involves the use of reason alone, independent of experience.

OUR EXPERIENCE OF THE WORLD IS SPLIT INTO TWO FORMS

Kant thought that experiences come from intuitions (the results of direct sensing) and understanding (the ability to have and use concepts about things we sense). We wouldn't know what our intuitions meant without concepts. For example, we may see (sense) two walls of a building, but our mind uses concepts to mentally construct the complete building they form.

"**Morality** is not... the doctrine of how we may make ourselves **happy**, but how we may make ourselves **worthy** of happiness."

THE CATEGORICAL IMPERATIVE

Within a decade, Kant had published his second and third critiques: *Critique of Practical Reason* (1788) and *Critique of Judgment* (1790). He believed it was possible to develop a consistent moral system using reason. People should act in ways that could become universal laws, without aiming to achieve personal desires or motives.

NOUMENA AND PHENOMENA

Kant argued that the human mind is limited—it can experience and imagine only within certain limits. He described two worlds: that of phenomena (things we can sense and experience) and that of noumena (things-in-themselves, which exist outside our mind). No matter how hard we think or experience, there is no access to the noumenal world, which remains unknowable.

Kant helped develop the nebular hypothesis in astronomy, which states that the solar system formed from large clouds of gas.

You can NEVER know it ALL

WE ARE CONTINUALLY FINDING OUT MORE ABOUT THE UNIVERSE, BUT IT SEEMS THAT THERE IS ALWAYS MORE TO DISCOVER. IT MAY BE THAT THERE REALLY ARE NO LIMITS TO WHAT THERE IS TO KNOW. SOME PHILOSOPHERS HAVE ASKED IF WE ARE CAPABLE OF KNOWING EVERYTHING THERE IS TO KNOW, OR IF THERE ARE SOME THINGS WE CAN NEVER KNOW.

The limits of experience

With the major advances in scientific discovery after medieval times, it seemed that we could go on finding out about the universe until we knew everything there is to know—that the only limits to our knowledge were the limits of what exists in reality. But in his *Essay Concerning Human Understanding*, John Locke challenged this assumption, and showed that we are not capable of knowing some things. As an empiricist, he believed that at birth our minds are a "blank slate": we know nothing, and acquire all our knowledge from experience through our five senses. And because our only way of getting information about the world outside us is through our senses, there may be parts of reality that are forever hidden from us. For example, a blind person can smell flowers, feel the warmth of the sun, and hear the rain, but can't see the moon or stars, and so can't have any direct firsthand knowledge of their existence. Our knowledge of reality is limited to what we can directly perceive, or to what we can infer based on what we can directly perceive (such as unobserved galaxies or electrons). But there may be much more to reality than we are capable of knowing in this way.

◐ The great unknown

Immanuel Kant argued that, no matter how hard we look, there will always be some things that are beyond our comprehension—things that are simply unknowable.

NO MAN'S KNOWLEDGE HERE CAN GO BEYOND HIS EXPERIENCE.

JOHN LOCKE

ARE THERE PARTS OF REALITY THAT WILL ALWAYS REMAIN IN THE DARK?

Immanuel Kant didn't look too far for the unknown—in his whole life, he never left the province where he was born.

Limited faculties

Another philosopher who explored the idea that there are limits to what we can know was Immanuel Kant, in the 18th century. Like Locke, he recognized that our faculties—our senses and our ability to reason—are not comprehensive and limit what we can know. But Kant also showed that what we experience with our senses is not necessarily the same as what actually exists. Our minds give us a representation of a thing, similar to the way a video camera gives us an audio-visual representation of a scene—it is like reality, but it is not reality, and does not capture everything there is in that reality. And, of course, our experience may add things that are not really there (as in illusions).

Two different realities

Kant explained that there is a difference between things as they appear to us and what they actually are—what he called the "thing-in-itself." It is as if these two things exist in two different worlds. There is the world as we experience it with our limited faculties, which he called the phenomenal world, but there is also a world of "things-in-themselves," the noumenal world, which we are not capable of experiencing. The total of what we can apprehend, know, and understand, is limited by our faculties, but that doesn't mean that other things don't exist—just that we have no way of perceiving them. Our knowledge is limited to the phenomenal world, the world of space and time that we can experience, and the noumenal world of things as they really are will always be unknowable to us. What we are able to experience is never reality as it is in itself. There are things that we can never know, and we can't even have an idea of what it is that we don't know, since these things are literally beyond our understanding.

IT IS PRECISELY IN KNOWING ITS LIMITS THAT PHILOSOPHY EXISTS.

IMMANUEL KANT

See also: 24–25

UNKNOWN UNKNOWNS

Former secretary of defense Donald Rumsfeld referred to the limits of our knowledge when he said, "There are known knowns; there are things we know that we know. There are known unknowns; that is to say, there are things that we now know we don't know. But there are also unknown unknowns—there are things we do not know we don't know."

TRUTH?

TRUTH?

TRUTH?

Do we ever really know the **TRUTH**?

PHILOSOPHICAL INQUIRY CAN BE SEEN AS A SEARCH FOR TRUTH—BUT PHILOSOPHERS HAVE ALSO DEBATED HOW MUCH OUR IDEAS OF WHAT IS TRUE CORRESPOND TO WHAT ACTUALLY IS THE CASE. SOME THOUGHT THAT WE MAY NEVER KNOW FOR SURE, BUT THAT THERE ARE CERTAIN THINGS WE CAN ACCEPT AS TRUE.

See also: 32–33, 44–45

Valid explanations

Our thirst for knowledge is what drives philosophical inquiry, and it isn't satisfied until we have found something we believe is true. Philosophers have argued about whether we can ever know if something is really true or not. But in the late 19th century, American philosopher Charles Sanders Peirce questioned the importance of this kind of truth. He thought that a lot of philosophical debate could never come to a satisfactory conclusion about what is and isn't true, and that this is, in fact, irrelevant—most of the time, what we need is simply a satisfactory explanation. If we believe something, and it works for us, it doesn't matter if it is an accurate picture of reality. What matters is the consequences of believing it is true. Knowledge, he suggested, consists of a collection of these valid explanations, rather than things that we know for certain to be facts. Peirce's ideas about truth formed the basis for a school of philosophy known as pragmatism. Pragmatists believe that the purpose of philosophy is not to try to provide a true picture of the universe, but to help us live in it practically.

True—or useful?

Peirce's view that what we consider to be true is a collection of valid explanations was very different from the traditional idea that truth consists of facts that never change. For Peirce, the explanations we accept as true can be replaced if a better

> **TRUTH HAPPENS TO AN IDEA. IT BECOMES TRUE, IS MADE TRUE BY EVENTS.**
> WiLLiAM JAMES

TRUTH?

TRUTH?

⟵ Believe in the truth
The universe doesn't change, but what we believe to be true about it changes all the time. Pragmatists think that if a belief is useful and helps us live in the universe, it doesn't matter if it is true or not.

BELIEFS

some philosophers scorned pragmatists, accusing them of giving up on the search for truth.

THE TRUTH IS OUT THERE SOMEWHERE—BUT WE HAVE TO SEARCH FOR IT...

THE FOREST PATH
To explain pragmatism, William James told the story of a man lost in a forest. Tired and hungry, he comes across a path. The man can choose to believe that the path will lead him out of the forest to food and shelter, and follow it. Alternatively, he can believe that it doesn't, and stay where he is and starve. Whichever choice he makes, it will be proved to be true.

WE DO NOT SOLVE PHILOSOPHICAL PROBLEMS, WE GET OVER THEM.
JOHN DEWEY

explanation is found. This notion was taken up by another American philosopher, William James. He believed that something is true as long as it is useful to us. As soon as it loses its usefulness, it is no longer true. For example, for a long time people believed that Earth was at the center of the universe, but as astronomers observed the orbits of the planets, this view of the universe became unsatisfactory. A new explanation, with the sun as the center of the universe, became the accepted "truth." The universe hadn't changed; only the truths we know about it. These truths are different from facts, and we don't need to know if the truth we use corresponds to the facts. We only need to know if it works for us. It is the usefulness of our beliefs, and how we use them, James said, that makes them true.

Practical philosophy
The idea that truth and usefulness are interrelated is central to pragmatism. Peirce emphasized that we gain knowledge not from simply observing and thinking, but by doing things—actively testing the usefulness of our knowledge

and considering the implications of accepting something as true. Later philosophers, notably John Dewey, applied this aspect of pragmatism to the practical problems of everyday life, and especially to politics and education. Dewey advocated hands-on learning, rather than learning by rote, or repetition, since this encourages us to discover useful explanations of things and not simply accept secondhand knowledge. Pragmatism became an important movement in 20th-century philosophy, particularly in the United States. There, philosophers moved away from the abstract problems of European philosophy toward a more practical approach, adopting Dewey's test of a successful philosophical theory: "Does it help us understand our experience, or make it more puzzling?"

Aristotle's belief that all of our knowledge comes from experience led him to study the natural world in detail, and then organize his findings. This formed the basis for modern taxonomy, in which organisms are classified into groups such as class, order, family, genus, and species.

NATURAL ORDER

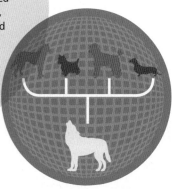

Philosophy and knowledge
IN PRACTICE

LIVE AND LEARN

Philosophical theories about how we acquire knowledge—through reasoning or experience—have influenced the development of learning theory in psychology. This, in turn, has formed the basis for modern theories of education, and especially the replacement of rote learning (through repetition) with more "hands-on" methods.

MAKING SENSE

The interaction between our minds and our senses is a major field of study in psychology (cognitive). It helps us understand the way our minds make sense of what our senses tell us (perception), and how they are sometimes deceived—for example, by optical illusions.

The science of genetics has raised the possibility that more of our behavior is due to inherited genetic factors than was previously thought, reviving the "nature versus nurture" debate. It has also been suggested that some abilities are innate, such as our ability to acquire and use language.

NATURE VERSUS NURTURE

Questions of knowledge, belief, and truth have a particular relevance in courts of law. Someone giving testimony swears to tell the truth, but only says what he or she believes to be true. It is up to the judge or jury to decide if a witness statement has been made in good faith, and whether or not it can be relied upon.

THE WHOLE TRUTH

The branch of philosophy concerned with knowledge, epistemology, has obvious links to psychology and the study of how we perceive and learn about the world around us. It also helps us make practical decisions in matters of truth and belief.

THE RIGHT POLICY

At election time, we can evaluate the policies of the different candidates by asking if these are based on experience or a rational argument, or are simply ideological, based on a strongly held belief. We can then make an informed vote.

What is
REALITY?

What is the UNIVERSE made of?

Is there a STRUCTURE to the universe?

What is REAL?

Is the world we know an ILLUSION?

How do you know anything EXISTS?

Is there a GOD?

SCIENCE doesn't have all the answers

What is TIME?

What's the point of my EXISTENCE?

Metaphysics developed from one of the earliest questions asked by philosophers: What is the universe made of? It is the area of philosophy that examines being—what actually exists and the nature of its existence, what it is like, and whether reality is made up of material substance, nonmaterial ideas, or a combination of both.

What is the **UNIVERSE** made of?

AS THE EARLIEST PHILOSOPHERS EXAMINED THE WORLD AROUND THEM, THEY REALIZED THAT THINGS THAT EXIST MUST BE MADE OF SOMETHING. THEIR FIRST QUESTION—"WHAT IS THE WORLD MADE OF?"—WAS THE BEGINNING OF A MAJOR BRANCH OF PHILOSOPHY, METAPHYSICS, WHICH IS CONCERNED WITH WHAT EXISTS, AND THE NATURE OF ITS EXISTENCE.

The substance of the universe

Miletus, a Greek coastal settlement in what is now Turkey, was the home of the earliest philosophers we know about. The first of these, Thales, was also an astronomer and engineer, who became fascinated by the question of what the universe is made of. He came up with a surprising theory, given the enormous variety of different things in the world: He believed that everything is composed of a single substance. This substance, he suggested, is water. He reasoned that water is necessary for all life, that land appears

> # EVERYTHING IS MADE OF WATER.
> THALES OF MILETUS

to emerge from the sea, and that water exists in liquid, gas, and solid forms; therefore, everything must consist of water at some point in its existence. Thales taught his new philosophical ideas to other thinkers, including Anaximander, who pointed out that if Earth is supported by water, there must be something that supports the water. Following Anaximander came yet more philosophers, offering alternative explanations, such as Anaximenes's theory that Earth floats on air, and that air must therefore be the single substance of the universe.

Something and nothing

Monism, the view that the universe essentially consists of a single substance, dominated early philosophy, and along with it came the idea that the fundamental nature of the universe is something that

LASTING IDEAS

Early Greek philosophy had a lasting influence. Empedocles's notion of four basic elements evolved into modern chemistry, which uses the term *element*. Modern physics shares the ideas and words of the atomists' theory of particles. Even the suggestion that everything is ultimately made of one substance has resurfaced in modern physics, with the idea that all matter is energy.

... OR FOUR ELEMENTS...

... OR COUNTLESS TINY PARTICLES?

IS THE UNIVERSE MADE OF...

... ONE SUBSTANCE...

◑ One, four, or many?

Early philosophers reasoned that the universe was made entirely of water, or from all four elements, or tiny atoms. Some of these early ideas are still being debated today.

does not change. Parmenides used reasoning to show that this must be the case. He argued that it is impossible for something both to exist and not exist, so we can't say that a state of nothing exists—there is no such thing as "nothing." Therefore, a thing that exists cannot have come from nothing—it must have always existed, and it will always exist since it can't become nothing either. The universe, then, must be full of something, since there is no "nothing." This "something" is a single substance that is unchanging and eternal.

Elements and atoms

Parmenides provided an interesting argument for the fundamentally unchanging nature of the universe, but there were others who disagreed. One, Empedocles, felt that Parmenides's theory could not explain the

Thales successfully predicted a solar eclipse. we still don't know how he did it.

variety of different things we can see in the world, or why the world appears to be constantly changing. Instead, he suggested that rather than one fundamental substance, there are four, which he called elements: fire, water, earth, and air. While these are themselves unchanging, they combine in different proportions to make the various things in the world, and the combinations change continually. Another theory, proposed by Democritus and Leucippus (known as the atomists), was that everything is composed of minuscule, unchanging, and indestructible particles called atoms. These are free to move around in completely empty space and combine with one another to form the various substances we find in the world. When these substances die or decay, the atoms recombine to form something new.

See also: 42–43, 66–67

> **NOTHING EXISTS EXCEPT ATOMS AND EMPTY SPACE; EVERYTHING ELSE IS OPINION.**
> **DEMOCRITUS**

ARISTOTLE'S FOUR CAUSES

→ The material cause
Everything is made of something. One such material, which we use to make things such as furniture, is wood. Wood is gathered from trees.

→ The formal cause
Next, something has to be put together in a certain way—it must have a form. This plan shows how wood can be put together to make a chair.

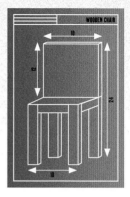

WOODEN CHAIR

Is there a **STRUCTURE**

WE LIVE IN A COMPLEX AND CONSTANTLY CHANGING UNIVERSE, WHICH EARLY PHILOSOPHERS TRIED TO MAKE SENSE OF BY ASKING WHAT EVERYTHING IS MADE OF. THEY ALSO WONDERED IF THE UNIVERSE IS AS CHAOTIC AS IT SEEMS. COULD THE UNIVERSE AND EVERYTHING IN IT HAVE AN UNDERLYING STRUCTURE? IF SO, WHAT CAUSED IT—AND DOES IT HAVE A PURPOSE?

Mathematics rules!
From the beginnings of philosophy, it has been suggested that there is an identifiable structure beneath the complexity of the world. Thales and his pupils proposed various models of the world as they knew it, either as a land floating on an infinite sea, or as a drum-shaped or flat disk suspended in air. Later explanations extended to the entire cosmos. People

MAN IS A UNIVERSE IN MICROCOSM.
DEMOCRITUS

HEAVENLY HARMONY
Pythagoras experimented with vibrating strings of different lengths and discovered a mathematical relationship between notes in a musical scale. He reasoned that the distances of heavenly bodies from Earth correspond to lengths of string that vibrate in harmony with one another, creating what he called a "harmony of the spheres" in space.

had discerned patterns in the movements of the sun, moon, planets, and stars, but the philosopher Pythagoras interpreted them differently. Fascinated by mathematics, he discovered that geometric shapes conform to particular mathematical rules, and reasoned that the shapes formed by the heavenly bodies would, too. He also found that musical notes that sound harmonious together correspond to a pattern of mathematical ratios (see Heavenly harmony, left). Pythagoras concluded that everything in the universe, including the positions and movement of the heavenly bodies, is governed by the rules of mathematics, and that the structure of the universe can be described in mathematical terms.

⊘ The efficient cause
For something to change, an outside agency or event must bring it about. In this case, a carpenter is shaping wood to follow the plan for a chair.

⊘ The final cause
Everything is made for a reason, and this is the final cause—the purpose of something. This chair has been made so that someone can sit down.

to the universe?

Atomic ideas

While Pythagoras looked for structure through mathematics and astronomy, other philosophers examined things on a smaller scale. Empedocles sought an explanation of the structure of everything from the way that different substances are formed from various combinations of fire, water, earth, and air. And the atomists Democritus and Leucippus described a universe made up of an infinite number of particles of various types and shapes. Every substance in the universe, including living beings as well as inanimate objects, is composed of these atoms, and the structure of everything is determined by their natural tendency to combine in certain ways. The atomists believed, unusually for the time, that because atoms are unchanging and eternal, they and the structures they create were not caused by anything and have no purpose.

Four causes

For many philosophers, it was not enough to say that the universe has a structure—it was necessary to explain how it came to be and for what purpose. Aristotle was concerned about identifying what he called the "causes" of things, but his use of the word *cause* is slightly different from our everyday meaning. What he called the "material cause" of something is the substance it is made from, while the "formal cause" is the way it is put together, its form or structure, which Aristotle believed followed certain natural principles and laws. The "efficient cause" is closest to our everyday meaning of *cause*: it is what brings about change, makes something come about, or change from one thing to another. The "final cause" of a thing, according to Aristotle, is the reason why it has come about and what it is for—its purpose. For anything to come about, he argued, these four causes must exist at the same time.

Before philosophers came along, the movements of the sun, moon, planets, and stars were associated with gods.

See also: 40–41

NUMBER IS THE RULER OF FORMS AND IDEAS.
PYTHAGORAS

What is REAL?

WHEN WE TALK ABOUT WHAT EXISTS, WE FIRST TEND TO THINK OF PHYSICAL OBJECTS THAT HAVE MATERIAL SUBSTANCE. BUT THERE ARE ALSO SEEMINGLY NONMATERIAL THINGS SUCH AS IDEAS, THOUGHTS, AND MEMORIES. WE CANNOT SEE OR TOUCH THEM, BUT THAT DOESN'T MEAN THEY ARE NOT REAL. SO WHAT ACTUALLY IS REAL?

> A MENTAL WORLD, OR UNIVERSE OF IDEAS, REQUIRES A CAUSE AS MUCH AS A MATERIAL WORLD, OR UNIVERSE OF OBJECTS, DOES.
>
> DAVID HUME

A material world

The obvious answer to the question of what is real is the things that are made of some physical substance that we can see and touch. Some philosophers argue that reality consists only of things perceived with our senses, the material world. Materialists, as they are known, believe there is no such thing as a nonmaterial world—nothing exists in reality that is not material. Among the first to hold this view were Democritus and Leucippus, who argued that there is nothing in reality but atoms and empty space, and Epicurus, who developed their argument further to demonstrate the nonexistence of anything nonmaterial, including a soul. But it was not until much later that materialism became part of mainstream philosophy, when science rather than religion became the main source of knowledge of the world. This increasingly materialist outlook was taken up in the 19th century by German philosophers Ludwig Feuerbach and Karl Marx, who were more openly dismissive of traditional religious descriptions of nonmaterial worlds.

An ideal world

At the other extreme from materialism is the belief that reality is essentially nonmaterial—that nothing material exists in reality. This view, idealism, was most convincingly proposed by George Berkeley. He argued that what we perceive are not material things in a physical world, but ideas in our minds. So reality consists only of ideas and the minds that perceive them, and there is no such thing as material substance. For an idea to exist, it has to be perceived. But if something exists only when it is perceived, does it cease to exist when there is no mind to perceive it? If a tree is growing in a park, for example, and there is nobody there to perceive it, is it still there? Berkeley, a Christian bishop,

MATERIAL WORLD
THIS WORLD CONTAINS THINGS THAT WE PERCEIVE WITH OUR SENSES. EVERYTHING IN THIS WORLD HAS A MATERIAL SUBSTANCE.

See also: 18–19, 20–21

DO THINGS EXIST...

said yes, the tree is still there: Things continue to exist because they are always perceived by the mind of God.

Total reality

Most philosophers, however, accept the existence of the material world, but also acknowledge the reality of nonmaterial things. Plato's notion that the everyday world we live in is just a "copy" of the real world of ideas was adopted by Christian and Islamic philosophers, and all the major religions contrast the earthly realm with another, ideal world. René Descartes, too, described total reality as consisting of two separate worlds, a material and an ideal world, and even the skeptical Hume did not deny the reality of nonmaterial things. Perhaps the most influential description of reality was provided by Immanuel Kant, who proposed that we can experience a world of things both material and nonmaterial with our senses and our minds, but this is only a part of total reality—there are also things we can't have any knowledge of, but which nevertheless exist in reality.

In everyday terms, a materialist is a person who values physical possessions and comforts over spiritual ideals.

> I AM SERIOUSLY PERSUADED THAT THERE IS NO SUCH THING AS WHAT PHILOSOPHERS CALL **MATERIAL SUBSTANCE.**
> GEORGE BERKELEY

JOHNSON'S PROOF

Most people instinctively feel that George Berkeley's notion that a material world does not exist cannot be true, but his argument for idealism is difficult to counter. The writer Samuel Johnson, however, offered a common-sense reply to Berkeley by forcefully kicking a large stone so that his boot bounced back from it, and saying, "I refute it thus."

IDEAL WORLD
THIS WORLD CONSISTS OF IDEAS, WHICH WE PERCEIVE WITH OUR MINDS. NOTHING IN THIS WORLD HAS A MATERIAL SUBSTANCE.

LOVE

TRUTH

TIME

... IF THEY DON'T HAVE A MATERIAL FORM?

Is the world we know an ILLUSION?

FROM THE TIME OF THE FIRST GREEK PHILOSOPHERS, IT HAS BEEN CLEAR THAT OUR KNOWLEDGE OF THE WORLD IS AT BEST INCOMPLETE, AND WE ARE OFTEN MISTAKEN. WE FORM AN IMPRESSION OF WHAT'S IN THE WORLD THROUGH OUR EXPERIENCE AND REASONING, BUT PHILOSOPHERS DISPUTE HOW ACCURATE A REPRESENTATION OF REALITY WE CAN ACHIEVE.

John Locke fled from England for five years when his ideas clashed with those of the king.

See also: 16–17, 20–21, 24–25

False impressions

Many philosophers have argued that what we experience through our senses—what we see, hear, smell, taste, and touch—gives us a false idea of what exists in reality. Plato explained that this is because the world we live in is actually only an illusory version of a perfect reality that we can't experience with our senses, an immaterial world of ideas we experience with our minds. The idea that there are two worlds, experienced in different ways, was also central to René Descartes's rationalist philosophy. Unlike Plato, however, he did not think of the material world as a "shadow" of an ideal reality. It is not the world that is imperfect, but our senses, which can be deceived and cannot be trusted to give us a true idea of the world around us. More reliable is our ability to reason, with which we can experience the ideal world and get a better understanding of things as they actually are.

The qualities of an object

Others, however, rejected the notion of an ideal, immaterial world. For empiricist philosophers, reality consists only of the material world we live in—the world that we experience through our senses. We use our reason to interpret what our senses tell us, and it is this that provides the ideas we have about the world. One such empiricist was John Locke, who suggested that we experience the material world in two ways. The objects of our experience, he said, have different

THERE ARE **TWO WORLDS**: THE WORLD OF **EXPERIENCE** SENSED BY OUR BODIES AND THE WORLD **AS IT IS IN ITSELF.**

IMMANUEL KANT

⬙ Two worlds, one mind

Arthur Schopenhauer believed that reality consists of a natural force that our will is a part of, and material objects that we experience through our senses.

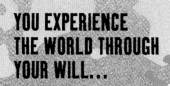

YOU EXPERIENCE THE WORLD THROUGH YOUR WILL...

... WHILE YOU OBSERVE A REPRESENTATION OF THE WORLD

OUR **WORLD**, WHICH IS SO **REAL**, WITH ALL ITS SUNS AND MILKY WAYS, IS—**NOTHING.**
ARTHUR SCHOPENHAUER

Where there's a Will...

Immanuel Kant proposed an explanation that combined rationalist and empiricist ideas, rejecting the notion of separate worlds we can experience either through our senses or our minds. He believed that we naturally know the properties of objects that exist in space and time, and we use this knowledge to interpret what our senses tell us. Another world exists, he said, of things-in-themselves, but this world is beyond our capability to experience. Arthur Schopenhauer agreed that reality consists of worlds we can and can't experience. He realized that we experience our own bodies as objects in the world, but we are also aware of our intentions, which cause those bodies to move and do things—our will, which is an example of a thing-in-itself. He concluded that reality consists of the material world, which he called the world of Representation, and an underlying force of nature, the world of Will. We can't experience the world of Will directly, but we are conscious of our own will, which is a part of the universal Will present in everything.

qualities. An object's "primary qualities," as he called them, are the properties that can be measured objectively, such as its size, weight, position, and movement—properties that are independent of the person observing them. Objects also have "secondary qualities," which can differ from one observer to another and are subjective—for example, the properties of taste, smell, and color. We can have an accurate experience of the primary qualities of an object, but our ideas of its secondary qualities are different from the object as it is in itself.

EAST MEETS WEST

Arthur Schopenhauer's idea that our will is part of a universal Will is similar to the concept of reality in Indian philosophy. Underlying Hinduism and Buddhism is the view that the world we experience is illusory and masks our perception of the eternal, universal reality that everything is part of. Only through enlightenment can we break the cycle of birth and rebirth and perceive this universal realm of being—the reality where all is One.

PLATO

c. 420–347 BCE

Born in the Greek city-state of Athens, Plato's early life is not well known. He is believed to have studied poetry and music, wrestled at the Isthmian Games at Corinth, and served in the Athenian army. With his well-connected family, Plato may have been destined for a life in Ancient Greek politics before he became a pupil of Socrates.

A LEGACY OF SOCRATES

Plato was greatly influenced by his teacher. After Socrates's death in 399 BCE, Plato abandoned public life in Athens and traveled widely, visiting Italy, Egypt, and Libya. When he began producing his own philosophical texts, he never referred to himself directly. Instead, he wrote dialogues, recording the types of conversations Socrates and others had in public.

THE ACADEMY

Plato returned to Athens in 387 BCE and founded the Academy, a school where a wide range of subjects, including astronomy and philosophy, were studied. Students included Aristotle, Xenocrates, and a handful of women such as Axiothea of Phlius. Plato left the school to his nephew, Speusippus, after which the Academy continued for more than 300 years.

THE WORLD OF PERFECT FORMS

One central idea in Plato's work is the world of forms, which are perfect and eternal versions of the things that we experience directly in our imperfect world. He illustrated this concept with the story of men chained and facing a cave wall with the sun, representing truth, behind them. The men see only shadows of the truth, which they believe form reality.

The legend of the lost city of Atlantis was first told by Plato in two of his dialogues, *Timaeus* and *Critias*.

> "The **price** good men pay for indifference to public affairs is to be **ruled** by **evil** men."

THE REPUBLIC

Plato had a great impact on Western philosophy, producing more than 30 dialogues. Written around 380 BCE, *The Republic* is one of Plato's most famous works. It considers the nature of justice, how individuals can be virtuous, and what the ideal state would be like. He also argues that a just life is connected to a happy life.

How do you know

IN TRYING TO ESTABLISH WHAT DOES OR DOES NOT EXIST, SEVERAL PHILOSOPHERS TOOK AS THEIR STARTING POINT THOUGHT EXPERIMENTS THAT DENIED WE CAN BE SURE OF ANYTHING EXCEPT OUR OWN EXISTENCE. FROM THIS SINGLE CERTAINTY, THEY BUILT ARGUMENTS FOR OUR KNOWLEDGE OF THE EXISTENCE OF OTHER THINGS.

See also: 18–19

The flying man

The Islamic philosopher Ibn Sînâ, also known as Avicenna, devised an intriguing image for his "flying man" thought experiment in the 11th century. He imagined a man floating in the air, blindfolded, and touching nothing, so that he receives no information from his senses and is completely unaware of his body or the world outside him. Yet he is still aware that he exists. Avicenna had set out to show that this thing that exists is the man's soul, distinct from his body.

According to Avicenna's account of his life, he had read and memorized the entire quran by the age of ten.

However, at the same time, he raised questions about what we can be sure exists other than ourselves. Around 600 years later, René Descartes presented a similar thought experiment—the idea of an evil demon deceiving all his senses—in order to dismiss anything that could be doubted, and build his knowledge of the world from the single certainty that he existed. But Avicenna and Descartes showed only that the "soul" or "mind" exists and is aware of its own existence, and not that they had bodies that exist in a material world.

A brain in a vat

In the 1980s, American philosopher Hilary Putnam took these thought experiments and presented an updated version, which raises similar questions about how much we can know about what really exists. Let us suppose, he said, that I don't exist in the way I think I do; instead, I am part of

ARE YOU REALLY EXPERIENCING LIFE, OR ARE YOU JUST A BRAIN IN A VAT?

◑ Wired to the world

Hilary Putnum described a thought experiment in which we exist as a brain in a vat, wired to a computer that makes us think we're experiencing the world outside.

anything **EXISTS**?

**COGITO ERGO SUM
(I THINK, THEREFORE I AM).**

RENÉ DESCARTES

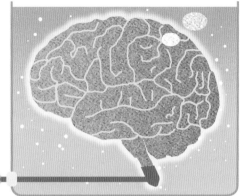

an experiment by a scientist who has removed my brain and put it in a vat to keep it alive. My brain is wired up to a computer that stimulates it, making me think I'm experiencing everything in the world, but in fact it is just a series of electrical signals. Every experience would be the same as if I experienced it with a real body in a real world—and I would have no way of knowing that this isn't the case. In Putnam's thought experiment, an external world exists (the scientist, the computer, and the brain in a vat), but I know nothing about it—only the illusions of a world that my brain is being given.

We can't be sure
Descartes and Putnam merely adopted a skeptical approach as a starting point to establish how we can know we exist,

but many philosophers have found the situations these thought experiments describe convincing. The evil demon and the brain in a vat are powerful images, and it is difficult to find any reason not to believe that they describe reality—but then how can we even know that the world we experience exists? Until we have a definitive answer, philosophers will continue to debate this question.

THE MATRIX
The *Matrix* trilogy of science-fiction movies brought the simulated-reality thought experiment into popular culture. In the movies, a breed of sentient computers control the minds of humans through implants, tricking them into believing in a virtual world totally different from the real world of their captivity.

Is there a **GOD**?

IN TRYING TO UNDERSTAND THE SUBSTANCE AND STRUCTURE OF THE UNIVERSE AND WHAT IT MEANS FOR SOMETHING TO EXIST, PHILOSOPHERS HAVE CONSIDERED HOW ANYTHING HAS COME TO BE. MANY BELIEVED THAT A GOD CREATED THE UNIVERSE, AND HAVE PROVIDED ARGUMENTS TO ATTEMPT TO PROVE HIS EXISTENCE.

Cause and purpose

Many of the arguments for the existence of a supreme being that created the universe date back to the philosophy of Plato and Aristotle. These arguments were adopted later by Christian philosophers in their attempts to reconcile their faith with philosophical reasoning. One of the major questions about existence is why anything exists at all. It seems wrong to assume that the universe came into existence on its own, so it must have been created—there must be a cause for it. The obvious objection is that this cause must itself have a cause, and so on, but philosophers using this "cosmological argument" said there is a first, uncaused cause, which we understand to be God. A different argument, the "teleological argument," or argument from design, points to the fact that we can detect definite patterns in the universe. For instance, Earth moves in a predictable course, and a cygnet will grow up to become a swan. These patterns indicate that the universe has been carefully designed, and therefore must be the work of a creator with some purpose, namely God.

> SOMETHING EXISTS THAT IS THE CAUSE OF THE **EXISTENCE** OF ALL THINGS, AND OF THE **GOODNESS** AND OF EVERY **PERFECTION** WHATSOEVER—AND THIS WE CALL **GOD**.
>
> **THOMAS AQUINAS**

THE PROBLEM OF EVIL

The fact that there is evil in the world is used to argue that there is no omnipotent (all-powerful) and benevolent God. If a good God is willing to prevent evil, but is unable to do so, he is not omnipotent. If he is able but not willing, he is not benevolent. If he is neither willing nor able, then there is no reason to regard him as God.

ACCORDING TO THESE ARGUMENTS...

TELEOLOGICAL
THE UNIVERSE AND EVERYTHING IN IT HAS BEEN DESIGNED ACCORDING TO A SPECIFIC PLAN OR PURPOSE. THIS DESIGNER IS GOD.

A perfect being

The medieval Christian philosopher Thomas Aquinas identified five arguments to prove God's existence, which he called the *Quinque viæ* ("Five Ways"). He took the teleological argument and three versions of the cosmological argument from Plato and Aristotle, but found the fifth "way" in the work of 11th-century theologian St. Anselm. Anselm defined God as a being so great that nothing greater can be conceived. We can imagine such a perfect being, so God exists as a concept in our minds—but a perfect being that exists in reality would clearly be even greater than one that exists only in our minds. So, we can now imagine a being greater than our initial idea of God, which exists in both our minds and reality. Such a being, God, must therefore exist: To deny his existence would contradict Anselm's definition of God.

> Thomas Aquinas believed that all living things have souls—even plants.

Not proved

Not everyone was convinced by these arguments, however, and even some who believed in the existence of God questioned their strength. Anselm's "ontological argument," although apparently logically sound, presupposes that we can conceive of the greatest conceivable being—which perhaps we cannot. The cosmological argument assumes that everything must have a cause, and that the cause that causes all other causes can only be God, but why suppose this? The argument from design is equally inconclusive, and suggests, rather than proves, the existence of a purposeful creator. By the 19th century, more and more philosophers were adopting a skeptical attitude toward belief in God. There was a growing consensus of opinion that because it is impossible to conclusively prove or disprove the existence of God, it should remain a matter of faith rather than philosophy.

See also: 112–113, 140–141

GOD IS THAT THAN WHICH NOTHING GREATER CAN BE THOUGHT.

ST. ANSELM

... THERE IS A GOD.

ONTOLOGICAL
WE CAN IMAGINE THE GREATEST, MOST PERFECT BEING IN OUR MINDS, SO THAT BEING, GOD, MUST ALSO EXIST IN REALITY. THEREFORE, GOD EXISTS.

COSMOLOGICAL
THE UNIVERSE COULDN'T JUST HAVE COME INTO BEING BY ITSELF, OUT OF NOTHING. IT MUST HAVE BEEN CREATED BY SOMETHING—BY GOD.

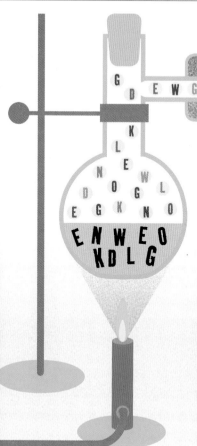

SCIENCE
doesn't have all the answers

MANY OF THE ORIGINAL QUESTIONS ABOUT THE UNIVERSE SEEM TO HAVE BEEN ANSWERED BY SCIENCE, AND NEW SCIENTIFIC DISCOVERIES FURTHER EXPLAIN THE WORLD AROUND US. IT SEEMS, HOWEVER, THAT THERE IS ALWAYS MORE TO DISCOVER, AND THERE MAY ALWAYS BE SOME QUESTIONS THAT SCIENCE CANNOT ANSWER.

Francis Bacon was an advisor to both Queen Elizabeth I and King James I of England.

Scientific method

Western philosophy began with questions about the physical universe—what it is made of and how it is structured. Philosophers proposed increasingly sophisticated theories to explain the natural world by using their ability to reason, developing logical arguments based on what they observed around them. This process of observation and reasoning, which was first formally recognized as a method of inquiry by Aristotle, evolved into "natural philosophy," what we now call science. The 16th century saw a number of scientific breakthroughs, such as Copernicus's theory of a universe revolving around the sun and Vesalius's investigations into human anatomy, which firmly established science rather than religion as the source of our knowledge of the natural world. But it was the philosopher Francis Bacon who realized that rather than simply observing that something appears to be the case, and concluding that it is so in every case, it was necessary to provide a reliable framework—a scientific method for testing new theories by experimentation.

ALL METHODOLOGIES, EVEN THE MOST OBVIOUS ONES, HAVE THEIR LIMITS.
PAUL FEYERABEND

Scientific progress

Armed with the authority of a scientific method, scientists made discoveries and proposed theories in a period sometimes called the Scientific Revolution. Science discovered some underlying principles of the universe: the laws of physics, chemistry, and the

WE LOOK FOR KNOWLEDGE THROUGH METHODS.

See also: 84–85, 100–101

> ONLY WHEN THEY MUST CHOOSE BETWEEN **COMPETING THEORIES** DO SCIENTISTS BEHAVE LIKE PHILOSOPHERS.
>
> THOMAS KUHN

Knowledge testing ⊙
Whenever possible, scientists subject theories to rigorous tests. If a theory repeatedly fails such tests, it will need to be altered or replaced by a better one.

living world. New discoveries produced new theories, each more sophisticated than the ones before. Sometimes, a breakthrough discovery or theory may mean a complete change in thinking—what the philosopher Thomas Kuhn calls a "paradigm shift." Turning points like this, such as the move from Newtonian to Einsteinian physics, characterize the way that science progresses, giving us an increasingly complete knowledge of scientific truth. But Paul Feyerabend suggested that each time such a shift occurs, the concepts and methods used change too, so there is no permanent framework for establishing this truth.

Unanswered questions
The progress of science from the Scientific Revolution onward has prompted a change in the emphasis of philosophical thinking. As the questions about the substance and structure of the universe were increasingly answered by physics and chemistry, philosophers focused more on the nature and meaning

of existence than its physical makeup. More recently, psychology and neuroscience have provided great insights into our behavior, the working of our minds, and how we acquire knowledge. But science does not, and cannot, explain everything. It provides us with increasing knowledge of the physical world and our mental world, but questions of morality and the meaning of our existence will, it seems, always be outside the scope of science.

THE BIG BANG
Often, scientific explanations raise yet more questions. Science has provided us with the theory that the Big Bang was the beginning of the universe. We instinctively ask the questions "What came before that?" or "What caused it?" But physicists explain that literally nothing, not even time, existed before that, challenging once again our philosophical ideas of the nature of existence.

THOMAS AQUINAS

(c. 1225–1274)

The youngest of nine children born to an Italian count, Thomas Aquinas was placed in the Monte Cassino monastery when he was just five. He later studied at the University of Naples and in Paris, where he was called "a dumb ox" for his silence during class. However, Aquinas was busily absorbing information and would become one of the Catholic Church's most important theorists.

KIDNAPPED!

In Naples, Aquinas became influenced by the Dominicans, a religious order who studied hard and helped the poor. His family disapproved, and kidnapped him in 1243. He was held prisoner for more than a year while they tried to change his mind. Finally, his family admitted defeat, and Aquinas was allowed to escape. He returned to the Dominicans and was sent to Paris.

Considered the Church's greatest scholar of the time, Aquinas was canonized (made a saint) in 1323 by Pope John XXII.

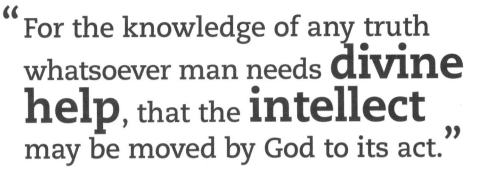

"For the knowledge of any truth whatsoever man needs **divine help**, that the **intellect** may be moved by God to its act."

LIFELONG LEARNING

As a member of the Dominican order, Aquinas embarked on a lifetime of learning, teaching, and writing. His output was vast for the time—more than 60 works, including the huge *Summa Theologica*, made up of thousands of pages handwritten by scribes, which sought to answer a wide range of questions about God and the Church.

THE UNIVERSE HAS NOT ALWAYS EXISTED

Aquinas was partly responsible for popularizing Aristotle's works in medieval Europe, reading translations from Arabic and writing commentaries on them. He even referred to Aristotle as "the Philosopher" throughout his *Summa Theologica*. Yet Aquinas didn't adopt all of Aristotle's theories, particularly disagreeing with the idea that the universe and earth did not have a beginning and were eternal.

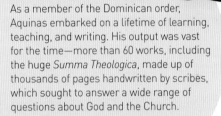

FAITH AND REASON CAN BE RECONCILED

Aquinas lived at a time when the Church and theology clashed with science and philosophy. Many people saw no place for philosophy in Christianity, especially that of non-Christians such as Aristotle. Aquinas believed that as "both kinds of knowledge ultimately come from God." both can work together to help each other.

What is TIME?

IN THE MODERN WORLD, WE ARE ESPECIALLY AWARE OF TIME PASSING.
WE EXPERIENCE THE CHANGING SEASONS AND THE PASSING DAYS, AND WE
HAVE INVENTED WAYS OF MEASURING TIME, EVEN THOUGH IT IS DIFFICULT
TO DEFINE. WE ALSO EXPERIENCE TIME AS A FUNDAMENTAL ASPECT OF
OUR EXISTENCE AS WE PASS THROUGH LIFE.

> **NOTHING ENDURES BUT CHANGE.**
> HERACLITUS

See also: 46–47

Existence and change

Early philosophers looking at
the world around them saw
a seemingly complex universe
in which things were constantly
changing over time. In trying
to understand the nature of
reality, they sought some
stability—to find the things
that were eternal and unchanging.
Change in the world was something to
be explained: for example, in terms of
the combining and recombining of
immutable, unchanging elements or
atoms. Heraclitus, however, accepted that
the universe is changing constantly, but
said that the things that were previously
considered eternal and unchanging are,
in fact, in a "state of flux." He explained
that, just as we can't step in the same
stream twice due to its continual flow,
we cannot experience the world in
the same way at different times.
Reality, according to Heraclitus,
consists not of things or
substances that are subject
to change, but of processes
that happen over time.

> Kant said space and time are "irremovable goggles" and part of the mind's organizing system.

Conscious of time

Many centuries later, Immanuel Kant
explained reality in terms of a world of
"things-in-themselves," which is outside
space and time, unlike the world we
experience. Although we live in a world of
space and time, Kant said that we do not
experience time directly, but get a sense
or impression of time only from the things

BACK TO THE FUTURE

Theories in physics suggest that
time travel may be possible. This
raises interesting philosophical
problems about the nature of time,
and also of existence and identity.
For example, if I traveled to the past
and killed my grandfather before
my father was born, it would mean
that I never came to exist. And if I
visited my younger self, to warn
myself about the mistakes I made,
I would never make them.

> **REALITY IS A HISTORICAL PROCESS.**
> GEORG HEGEL

WE EXIST BOTH IN SPACE AND TIME.

in the world that change—such as day following night, or the flow of sand in an hourglass. But German philosopher Georg Hegel suggested that in addition to being conscious of time because of the things in the world that change, we are a part of the world we live in, so our consciousness itself is subject to change. We experience the passage of time as a historical process, in which the spirit of each period of time—the *Zeitgeist*—changes inevitably as new ideas emerge.

Our being is time

In the 20th century, French philosopher Henri Bergson, influenced by Charles Darwin's theory of evolution, regarded reality as an evolutionary process, a continuum, similar to Heraclitus's notion of a constantly shifting flow. He also argued that we have a direct inner experience of time, and that this is the essential nature of our existence. Martin Heidegger came to a similar conclusion, from a different perspective. We exist in the world of space and time, and in addition to being aware of our physical place in it, we are aware of not just our present, but a future and past too, and that our lives have a beginning and an end. We do not simply experience time—our being actually is time. Despite this influential view, some philosophers continue to argue that time is an aspect of human perception, rather than one of reality.

◑ The time of our lives
Just as we are aware of our place in the physical world—where we are in relation to other things in the universe—we are also aware of our place in time. We define our existence through the passing of time.

What's the point of my **EXISTENCE?**

PHILOSOPHERS EXAMINING QUESTIONS OF EXISTENCE INCREASINGLY TURNED FROM THE WORLD AROUND THEM TO OUR PLACE IN THAT WORLD. SOME EXAMINED THE NATURE OF HUMAN EXISTENCE—HOW WE EXIST AS INDIVIDUALS, AND WHETHER WE CAN FIND MEANING IN OUR LIVES.

We are free to choose

Although søren kierkegaard struggled to find meaning in life, he never lost his faith in god.

One of the best-known philosophers to look at what it means to exist as a human was Danish philosopher Søren Kierkegaard, in the 19th century. He believed that since many philosophical explanations of existence were at odds with our individual experience, we have the ability to make choices that shape our lives. We have the freedom, he argued, to make moral decisions about how we lead our lives, and it is this that can give our lives meaning. However, this freedom of choice does not necessarily bring us any happiness. On the contrary, when we realize that we are absolutely free to choose to do anything, our minds reel, and we have feelings of dread and anxiety. This "dizziness of freedom," as Kierkegaard called it, comes from an awareness of our own existence and personal responsibility.

See also: 32–33, 46–47, 58–59

We then have to decide whether this leads to despair and choosing to do nothing, or to living "authentically," making choices that give meaning to our lives.

Realizing potential

Other philosophers took up Kierkegaard's idea that we are free to shape our lives for ourselves. Friedrich Nietzsche, for example, argued it was up to each individual to realize his or her own potential, rather than follow decisions dictated by convention or religion. Later, Edmund Husserl took the view that if, as Immanuel Kant had argued, there is a world of things-in-themselves, separate from space and time, which we have no means of understanding or experiencing, any ideas we have of that world are simply speculation. We might as well ignore it for all practical purposes, and concentrate on the world as we experience it. Husserl called this the *Lebenswelt*—the world we live in. This subjective approach, concentrating on our own experience,

WHY ARE THERE BEINGS AT ALL, AND WHY NOT RATHER **NOTHING?** THAT IS THE **QUESTION.**

MARTIN HEIDEGGER

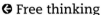

⊙ Free thinking
Some philosophers believe that individuals are free to do anything they want with their lives. We do not have to live within the constraints of our society.

WE ARE FREE TO FIND OUR OWN MEANING IN LIFE.

was then taken up by Martin Heidegger. Heidegger argued that philosophy has tried to find explanations of existence, but to understand existence we first need to examine ourselves and our own existence—what it means for us to exist.

The meaning of life

Heidegger's ideas were very influential on the next generation of philosophers, especially in France. The term *existentialism* was coined to describe the philosophy that emerged in the second half of the 20th century. This philosophy examined human existence—in particular, the search for meaning or purpose in life in a world that had increasingly rejected God and religion. Foremost among these philosophers was Jean-Paul Sartre, who said that we do not choose to exist—we are born into a world that we are bound to live in—but once we reach an awareness of our own existence, we have to create our own purpose in life to give it meaning. Albert Camus, who like Sartre was a novelist as well as a philosopher, was more pessimistic. He took the view that

there was essentially no purpose to be found in our lives, and to deal with the anxiety that comes from our self-awareness, we have a choice of either accepting the futility and absurdity of existence, or choosing not to exist at all.

MAN IS **CONDEMNED** TO BE **FREE;** BECAUSE ONCE THROWN INTO THE WORLD, HE IS **RESPONSIBLE** FOR EVERYTHING HE DOES.

JEAN-PAUL SARTRE

EXISTENTIAL ANGST

Søren Kierkegaard described the anxiety we feel when we become aware of our existence and the choices we can make—"existential angst"—as being similar to the feeling of standing on the edge of a cliff. We are anxious not only because we have a fear of falling, but also because we experience an impulse to throw ourselves off. We realize that only we can decide whether we jump or not.

SPACE AND TIME

The idea that atoms were the building blocks of the universe was first proposed by ancient Greek philosophers. Recent studies in quantum mechanics suggest that subatomic particles can move backward as well as forward in time, and can be in different places at once, making time travel theoretically possible.

SPACE AND TIME

Metaphysics
IN PRACTICE

IN THE BEGINNING

Scientists, like philosophers before them, have debated whether or not the universe has always existed. Recent theories, such as the Big Bang theory, suggest that the universe had a definite beginning, and that nothing, not even time itself, existed before then.

THAT'S LIFE

Our desire to understand the nature of things that exist has brought about sciences such as physics and chemistry, as well as the biological sciences, which examine living things. Genetics is getting ever closer to explaining life itself, and medical advances have even made it possible to repair genes and treat diseases.

There is a huge variety of things that exist in the world, both living and inanimate. From the attempt to understand the reason for this astonishing diversity, the science of ecology evolved, examining the interdependence of all living things and their environments.

LIFE ON EARTH

THE MEANING OF LIFE

Coming to terms with mortality and the apparent pointlessness of our existence can be traumatic, but existentialist philosophy has also influenced branches of psychotherapy that help us take responsibility for our actions and find a purpose in our lives.

Metaphysics, the branch of philosophy that is concerned with the nature of existence, poses questions about the world around us, which the natural sciences attempt to answer. But it also examines the reason for our existence, which can influence how we lead our lives.

OTHER WORLDS

Roughly three-quarters of the world's population have a religious belief, and most believe in some form of world outside the one we live in. Notions of an afterlife, heaven and hell, or the possibility of accessing another world through religious practices often shape how people live their lives.

What is the MIND?

Is there such a thing as an IMMORTAL soul?

Is your MIND separate from your BODY?

What is CONSCIOUSNESS?

ANIMALS have thoughts and feelings, too

Do you FEEL like I do?

What MAKES you YOU?

Can COMPUTERS think?

Can science explain how our MINDS WORK?

Philosophy of mind has its roots in the religious idea that we have an immortal soul that is responsible for thought, reasoning, and feelings. Some philosophers have argued that this, the mind, is separate from our physical body. This branch of philosophy also asks if we can know anything about other people's minds, and examines consciousness.

Is there such a thing as an IMMORTAL soul?

IT IS A CENTRAL BELIEF OF MANY RELIGIONS THAT IN ADDITION TO OUR PHYSICAL BODIES, WE HAVE A SOUL THAT LIVES ON AFTER DEATH. OPINION HAS BEEN DIVIDED AMONG PHILOSOPHERS, HOWEVER, AS TO THE EXISTENCE OF AN IMMORTAL SOUL. SOME HAVE ARGUED THAT WE DO HAVE A "SPIRIT," WHICH IS IMMATERIAL AND ETERNAL, WHILE OTHERS BELIEVED THAT THIS PERISHES WITH OUR PHYSICAL BODIES.

The eternal psyche

For much of the history of Western philosophy, few philosophers doubted that we have both physical and nonmaterial components to our existence. Where their beliefs differed, however, was in the nature of the nonmaterial part of our being. Socrates and Plato, for example, believed that humans possess both a physical body and a *psyche*, which corresponds to what we today call a soul, spirit, or mind. The psyche, according to Plato, is the true essence of a person, and consists of three elements: the *logos* (mind or reason), *thymos* (emotion or spirit), and *eros* (desire or appetite). Through our senses, our physical bodies experience the everyday world, but our psyches give us access to a perfect world, separate from the one we live in, which he called the world of ideas. The psyche is both eternal and immaterial, and Plato argued that our innate knowledge of this other world is a memory of our psyche from its existence before we were born. After our death, the psyche is reborn in other physical bodies.

Greek philosopher Empedocles jumped into a volcano to prove he was immortal. He perished.

Body and soul

Aristotle had a very different explanation of the psyche. For one thing, he thought that the psyche does not exist separately from the physical body, but is the essence of any living thing—the purpose of its being. All living things, not just humans, have some form of "soul" in this sense, ranging from the simple souls of plants whose psyches are characterized by their purpose of growing and reproducing,

ALL MEN'S SOULS ARE IMMORTAL.

SOCRATES

WHEN **DEATH** DOES COME, WE NO LONGER **EXIST.**

EPiCURUS

See also: 20–21, 46–47

through animals with more complex purposes in life, to human psyches that include intellect and emotion. The psyches of all living organisms are inseparable from their physical existence, and for Aristotle there can be no living organism without a psyche, nor a soul without a physical body. And since all living creatures are mortal, their psyches die with them.

It's a matter of faith

The word *soul* has a different meaning to us today from Aristotle's notion of psyche, and carries with it religious connotations. The idea of an immortal soul that lives on after death in another world is a central element in Christianity and Islam, and both religions incorporated Plato's and Aristotle's arguments for the existence of a psyche into their doctrines. In Eastern (especially Indian) philosophy, the idea of a

... BUT OUR SOULS LIVE FOREVER.

⊙ The spirit goes on
Plato's definition of the psyche encompassed ideas, emotions, and desires—what we now equate with the mind. Like many religions, he asserted that the soul lives on after we die.

OUR BODIES MAY FADE...

"self" continually going through a cycle of birth and rebirth, in which the soul is reincarnated in another physical body, is virtually taken for granted. Belief in an immortal soul, however, like belief in the existence of God, is ultimately a matter of faith rather than philosophy. But even if they rejected the idea of the immortality of the soul, many philosophers accepted that there may be more to our being than simply our physical bodies—a nonmaterial something, which we call the mind.

THE ATOMISTS

Among the first philosophers to dispute the immortality of the soul were the atomists Leucippus and Democritus. They didn't deny that we have a soul, but proposed that it, like everything else, is made of atoms, and that after death souls disperse and reform elsewhere as other things. Later, Epicurus argued that if nothing exists except atoms and empty space, there can be no such thing as a nonmaterial soul.

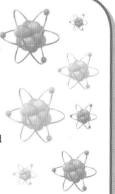

Is your **MIND**

WE EXPERIENCE THINGS WITH OUR SENSES, BUT ALSO HAVE THOUGHTS AND FEELINGS THAT ARE MENTAL RATHER THAN PHYSICAL. SOME PHILOSOPHERS HAVE CONCLUDED THAT WE HAVE A MIND, NOT MADE OF ANY MATERIAL SUBSTANCE, THAT EXISTS APART FROM OUR PHYSICAL BODY. OTHERS ARGUE THAT THE MIND IS AN INHERENT PART OF THE BODY.

> **IT IS CERTAIN THAT I AM REALLY DISTINCT FROM MY BODY, AND CAN EXIST WITHOUT IT.**
> RENÉ DESCARTES

See also: 26–27, 76–77

An independent mind

In an attempt to base his philosophy on only the things he could not doubt, René Descartes came to the conclusion that he could be sure of his existence as a thinking being—*cogito ergo sum* ("I think, therefore I am"). His senses, he realized, could be deceived, and since he associated these with his physical body, he concluded that the being that existed and was thinking must be independent of his body—a mind with no material substance. Our bodies, he added, are purely physical, and behave like machines, whereas our minds are capable of thinking and reasoning. This idea that our mind and body are two distinct things, known as mind-body dualism, has much in common with the religious notion that we have a soul. The mind that Descartes describes, however, is the realm of our mental, rather than spiritual, being.

A meeting of mind and body

A major problem of considering the mind and the body as separate and distinct entities is that the two obviously interact. If the body is simply a machine, its actions must be controlled by the mind. Similarly, for the mind to experience the external world, it must receive information from the senses. For a philosopher who accepts mind-body dualism, the obvious point of connection is in the brain, and Descartes went as far as to suggest that the interface between the two is the pineal gland, which he described as the "seat of the soul." But the Dutch philosopher Benedictus Spinoza suggested a different solution to this problem. He proposed that instead of consisting of a physical body

PHYSICALISM

A group of philosophers called physicalists believe that everything that exists in the world can be explained in physical terms. This does not mean that everything has a physical substance, but that our mental experiences, for instance, can be explained in terms of the physiology of our brains, or our disposition toward certain kinds of behavior. But physical events, they argue, must have physical causes, and a nonphysical mind could have no effect on the behavior of a physical body.

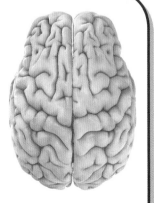

> **THE MIND IS PART OF GOD'S INFINITE INTELLECT.**
> BENEDICTUS SPINOZA

separate from your BODY?

MY MIND...

... CONTROLS
MY BODY.

⬆ Pulling the strings
René Descartes likened the body
to a machine, which is controlled
by a separate entity—the mind.
The mind receives information
from the senses via the brain and
processes it using reasoning.

and a nonmaterial
mind, we, and
everything in the
universe, are made
solely of a material
substance. That
substance, however,
has two distinct kinds
of properties—physical and
mental. In his "property dualism,"
as it became known, our physical
bodies (and, Spinoza believed,
all physical things—even rocks)
also have nonphysical, mental
attributes. For Spinoza, the idea
had religious significance, since
he believed that this one
material substance is God: God
is the universe and everything in
it, all of which has both mental
and physical properties.

psychology
evolved as a science
with the specific
purpose of studying
the mind.

A ghost in the machine
Some philosophers did not
accept the dualist idea of a
distinction between the mental
and physical. Especially in
the 20th century, there was a
feeling that mental events could
be explained in terms of the
physical workings of the brain.
English philosopher Gilbert Ryle
dismissed the idea of a separate
mind and body by saying that
we can be tricked into thinking
that a machine has a conscious
mind, when in fact it is just
doing the task it is designed
for. All we are seeing, he argued,
is a "ghost in the machine."
Similarly, what Descartes
regarded as a separate mind is
actually an integral part of our
physical bodies—the way that
they work and how they behave.

What is **CONSCIOUSNESS**?

AS HUMANS, WE CAN EXPERIENCE THE WORLD AROUND US THROUGH OUR SENSES, AND WE HAVE THOUGHTS AND FEELINGS. WE ARE ALSO AWARE OF HAVING THESE EXPERIENCES—WE ARE CONSCIOUS OF OUR SENSATIONS AND MENTAL PROCESSES. BUT CONSCIOUSNESS IS A PERSONAL THING, AND IT IS DIFFICULT TO DEFINE EXACTLY WHAT IT IS LIKE TO BE CONSCIOUS.

OUR THOUGHTS ARE ORGANIZED INTO A STREAM OF CONSCIOUSNESS...

Being aware of our existence

Almost all philosophers would acknowledge the existence of nonmaterial things such as thoughts and feelings. Even physicalists, who reject the notion of an immaterial mind that is separate from the body, recognize that we have ideas and perceptions, but argue that these can be explained in terms of the physical makeup of our bodies and brains. We are, however, all aware of these mental experiences, and conscious of having both a mental and physical existence. We have physical sensations—what we see, hear, smell, touch, and taste through our sense organs—and we are conscious of having them. We also have thoughts, memories, and feelings, which are purely mental. Our awareness of these mental phenomena, and perhaps more importantly our self-awareness, is what we experience as consciousness.

william James liked to go to seances, and was president of the british society for psychical research.

A bundle of sensations

The notion that consciousness is an awareness of sensations, thoughts, and feelings raises problems, however. It is impossible to examine consciousness objectively. I can only look at my own conscious mind, and I cannot have direct access to

THE **MIND** IS A KIND OF **THEATRE,** WHERE SEVERAL PERCEPTIONS SUCCESSIVELY MAKE THEIR APPEARANCE.

DAViD HUME

WITHIN EACH **PERSONAL** CONSCIOUSNESS, THOUGHT IS SENSIBLY CONTINUOUS.

WILLIAM JAMES

someone else's consciousness. I know what it is like for me to have a conscious experience, but not for someone other than myself. Our concepts of consciousness are necessarily subjective, and difficult to define further than a description of what it is like for each of us to be a conscious being. Yet we all have an idea of this "what-it's-likeness," and this is part of what gives us a feeling of self. Scottish philosopher David Hume suggested that we have thoughts, experiences, and memories—what he described as a "bundle of sensations"—that together form the subjective consciousness we recognize as our self.

A SCIENTIFIC APPROACH

Notions such as consciousness highlight one of the problems of the philosophy of mind, which is that we can only directly experience what is going on in our own minds. Because of this, it has a tendency to be subjective and introspective, and is considered to be unscientific. Scientists working in similar fields sought to give their investigations into the workings of the mind a more objective, scientific foundation, and from this emerged the new science of psychology.

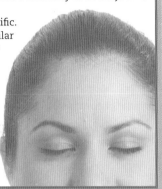

Continually changing consciousness

William James, a philosopher, but also one of the pioneers of psychology, attempted to give a more scientific explanation of consciousness. He recognized that our minds not only receive sensory perceptions from the external world around us, but also go through mental processes to interpret that information. We organize our thoughts and ideas about the things we experience, making connections between them and storing them in our memories. As we go through life, we are constantly experiencing new things, and these new perceptions prompt new thoughts and ideas. So, James said, consciousness should not be considered as a state of mind, but rather as a continually changing process. He called this a "stream of consciousness," which is personal to each of us.

See also: 82–83, 84–85

◑ Going with the flow

William James described consciousness as being like a stream—changing all the time. As we experience new things, our minds interpret the information and organize our thoughts accordingly.

RENÉ DESCARTES

1596–1650

The son of a French politician, René Descartes was brought up by his grandmother after his mother died. He earned a law degree at the age of 22, but found that, except for mathematics, his education taught him little of certainty. He never married, although he did have a daughter, Francine. He spent most of his life living modestly off his family inheritance and developing influential theories on reason and doubt.

VISIONS OF A WANDERER

Starting in 1618, Descartes spent a decade traveling through Europe. He joined the Dutch army, visiting Hungary, Bohemia (in the modern-day Czech Republic), France, and Italy. In 1619, he had three strange dreams that led him to believe that all of science could be understood by using reason. When he settled in the Netherlands, he never lived in one place for long, moving at least 18 times in 22 years.

Descartes was born in La Haye en Touraine, a settlement in central France that, in 1967, was renamed Descartes in his honor.

WITH ME, EVERYTHING TURNS INTO MATHEMATICS

Although he made breakthroughs in optics and other sciences, Descartes was primarily a philosopher and mathematician. He believed in breaking problems up into their simplest parts, and applied algebra to geometry, creating analytical geometry. He developed Cartesian coordinates to locate a point in space in three dimensions, which he explained in *La Géométrie* (1637).

> " If you would be a real seeker **after truth**, it is necessary that at least once in your life **you doubt**, as far as possible, all things. "

I THINK, THEREFORE I AM

Descartes cast doubt on the reliability of the human senses, as well as the opinions of experts. He devised a system, outlined in his *Discourse on the Method* (1637), in which everything was methodically doubted until it was fully proven. His first certainty was expressed in Latin as *cogito ergo sum*— "I think, therefore I am."

LATE RISER

As a child, Descartes suffered from ill health, so he was allowed to sleep until noon— a custom he continued throughout his life since he maintained he did his best thinking in bed. He broke with tradition from 1649 to 1650 when tutoring Queen Christina of Sweden, who insisted on meeting at 5 o'clock each morning. Sadly, these early starts didn't suit Descartes. He caught pneumonia and died.

ANIMALS have thoughts and feelings, too

UNTIL QUITE RECENTLY, MANY PHILOSOPHERS VIEWED HUMANS AS SOMEHOW DIFFERENT FROM OTHER ANIMALS BECAUSE OF THEIR SUPPOSED SUPERIOR POWERS OF REASONING. TODAY, HOWEVER, MOST PEOPLE RECOGNIZE THAT ANIMALS FEEL PAIN TOO, AND THAT MANY ANIMALS HAVE THE ABILITY TO REASON. ARE ANIMALS' MINDS REALLY SO DIFFERENT FROM OUR OWN?

I THINK, THEREFORE I AM.

Biological machines

In the Western world, from the time of the first Greek philosophers until the 19th century, it was generally believed that what distinguished humans from animals was the possession of an immortal soul. Even as philosophers shifted their attention away from the concept of a soul to thinking about the mind and our ability to reason, reasoning was considered a uniquely human ability. René Descartes, for example, argued that the mind is separate from the physical body, but only in humans. Animals, he believed, are incapable of reasoning and therefore have no minds— they are simply biological machines that behave like mechanical toys.

The human animal

The idea that animals are soulless, mindless creatures persisted widely until Charles Darwin challenged

⊛ Thoughtful paws
René Descartes believed that animals simply react to the stimulation of their senses, and do not think or feel. Later philosophers have argued that since humans themselves are animals, other animals must suffer in the same way.

conventional thinking with his theory of evolution. Among other things, this demonstrated that humans evolved as part of the natural world. With this came a growing realization that if we are simply another species in the world of animals, they may share characteristics that we had assumed were uniquely human. Attitudes toward animals changed rapidly, and the idea that they were conscious beings, capable of feeling, gained ground. This led to movements to prevent cruelty to and exploitation of animals, as people questioned the morality of blood sports and animal experimentation, and during the 20th century a growing number of people have insisted that killing animals for food is unethical.

Animal rights

As the view that at least some animals can feel pain became generally accepted, philosophers returned to questions of how much animals can be considered to think like us. Australian philosopher Peter Singer argued that if animals are able to experience pain, and we believe that it is wrong to inflict unnecessary pain, then it is morally wrong to subject them to unnecessary suffering. He suggested that animals, like humans, have natural rights to life and freedom from needless distress. The notion of animal rights was accepted only by a minority, however, and several criticisms

> True to his belief that it is morally wrong to inflict pain on animals, Peter Singer has been a vegetarian since 1971.

IN SUFFERING, ANIMALS ARE OUR EQUALS.
PETER SINGER

were leveled against it. For example, animals are often used in medical research, in order to find treatments to ease human suffering. In this case, it seems that our rights outweigh those of the animals. We also tend to place a higher value on the rights of mammals than on those of invertebrates: There is an outcry at the killing of baby seals, for instance, but we have no qualms about calling in exterminators to clear a house of termites. It has been suggested that when we talk of animal rights, we are guilty of anthropomorphism—projecting our own ideas and feelings onto animals. Some modern philosophers say that we should instead examine our own morality, especially in treating animals as a means to an end, as a source of food, or as subjects of our experiments.

See also: 66–67, 68–69

THE LOWER ANIMALS, LIKE MAN, FEEL PLEASURE AND PAIN, HAPPINESS AND MISERY.
CHARLES DARWIN

LAB RATS

One of the main reasons for animal experimentation is to avoid unethical trials causing pain and distress to human subjects. Psychologists have observed the behavior of rats, for example, to give an insight into the workings of the human mind. This assumes that their minds are similar to ours—but if they are, it raises the question of whether it is ethical to experiment on them. And if they are not, such experiments will tell us nothing about the human mind.

Do you **FEEL** like

WHEN WE INTERACT WITH OTHERS, WE TAKE IT FOR GRANTED THAT THEY HAVE THOUGHTS AND FEELINGS MUCH LIKE OURS. EACH OF US KNOWS WHAT IT IS LIKE TO EXPERIENCE PAIN OR PLEASURE, AND HOW WE REACT TO THOSE FEELINGS. BUT WE CAN'T LOOK INSIDE OTHER PEOPLE'S MINDS, SO HOW DO WE KNOW THEY THINK AND FEEL THE SAME WAY AS WE DO?

> **WHAT DO I SEE FROM THIS WINDOW BUT HATS AND COATS WHICH MAY COVER AUTOMATIC MACHINES?**
>
> RENÉ DESCARTES

See also: 70–71

It's a subjective experience

One of the big problems for philosophers considering the human mind is whether or not everyone experiences things in the same way. Philosophers such as René Descartes arrived at their theories of the mind largely through introspective thinking—examining their own minds and mental processes—and made the assumption that other people's minds work in much the same way. But some philosophers pointed out that the content of our minds is personal and hidden from everybody else—we have no direct access to it. We can only know directly what goes on in our own minds, and drawing conclusions from a single case is a shaky basis for any theory. What justification do I have for believing that my subjective experience of things such as pain and pleasure, and even my own consciousness, is the same as everyone else's?

NO one can "read" minds, but we can often find clues in other people's facial expressions.

Surely everyone feels pain?

There is a common-sense argument that backs up our intuitive feeling that other people's minds work in a similar way, using the evidence of their behavior. I know that when I hit my head on a door, for example, I experience the sensation of pain, and I respond with a certain kind of behavior, such as wincing, saying "ouch," or even swearing. When I see other people banging their heads and responding with similar behavior, I infer that they are experiencing pain, too. We recognize universal kinds of behavior, such as crying or laughing, and associate those instinctively with the subjective feelings we have that provoke the same reactions in us. Since we all show similar responses to external stimuli, is it not

I do?

reasonable to conclude that we all experience the same thoughts and feelings, and that our minds work in a similar way?

Maybe we're all different

But the common-sense argument still draws conclusions about other minds based on just a single observation—my own mind. How can I know that because everybody reacts in the same way to things, they are all feeling the same sensations? A woman shouting "ouch" after walking into a door may just be mimicking the behavior of someone in pain, and not actually experiencing the sensation. In the same way, something she sees as red may be what I see as blue.

❯ Locked in thought
We like to think we know what other people are thinking and feeling, but we cannot see directly into their minds. We must infer what they think and feel from their behavior.

PHILOSOPHICAL ZOMBIES

In philosophy, zombies are not the undead monsters of Hollywood films. Rather, they are people that look and behave like us, but who actually have no consciousness. If you hit a zombie, it reacts as we would, but feels no pain. Philosophers have used the concept of zombies to dispute the idea that all of human nature has purely physical causes: It is our conscious mental experience—our mind—that distinguishes us from zombies.

Because her inner experiences are hidden from me, I cannot know firsthand what she is feeling or seeing, but only infer this indirectly from her behavior or what she tells me. But perhaps this is enough: After all, we accept secondhand descriptions of faraway places without having personally experienced them.

EXPERIENCES

THOUGHTS

IDEAS

FEELINGS

MEMORIES

WHAT'S GOING ON IN YOUR MIND?

What MAKES

MY THOUGHTS...

EXPERIENCES...

BELIEFS...

AND MEMORIES MAKE ME, ME.

EACH OF US IS A UNIQUE INDIVIDUAL. WE EACH HAVE A PHYSICAL BODY THAT IS DISTINCT FROM EVERYBODY ELSE'S, BUT ALSO A "SELF"—A PERSONAL IDENTITY THAT INCLUDES OUR THOUGHTS, FEELINGS, AND MEMORIES. WE CHANGE A LOT, PHYSICALLY AND PSYCHOLOGICALLY, THROUGHOUT OUR LIVES, YET STILL FEEL WE HAVE THE SAME IDENTITY.

The ship of Theseus

There's an old joke about a carpenter who has had the same hammer for 50 years, and it's only had three new heads and two new shafts, which tells us something about our instinctive attitude toward identity. The philosopher Thomas Hobbes explored the ideas we have of personal identity as we change over time, using a similar story. Theseus, he said, went on a long sea voyage, and during the journey his ship needed extensive repairs. Gradually, every part of the vessel was replaced with a new part, but we still think of the ship that ended the voyage as the same ship, even though nothing of the original remained. The same thing happens to us as we go through life. Cells in our bodies are continually being replaced, so that after a few years we are physically completely different. Our ideas, thoughts, and feelings also change enormously, but we still believe we are still the same person.

Thomas Hobbes wasn't a fan of university philosophy lectures, bemoaning the "frequency of insignificant speech."

Identity crisis

Philosophers have puzzled over what identity is, but agree that it is the nonphysical part of our beings—the mind—that defines us. Our thoughts and beliefs may change as we age, but we remain essentially the same person.

you YOU?

Hardware and software

For philosophers like Hobbes, the problem is, if we change so much, what is it that makes up our personal identity? Is there a part of us that does not change? Unlike Theseus's ship, we are living beings, and have a single life. Our cells can be replaced, and we can even have organ transplants and still remain the same organism. But if it were possible to have a brain transplant, maybe that would mean a change of identity—we would view it as the brain taking on a new body, rather than the body accepting the brain as a new "spare part." So it may be that the brain is where our identity lies, but what is it that makes this particular physical organ different from, say, the heart? The answer seems to be that it is not the "hardware" of the brain, the physical cells, but something to do with the "software," what is going on inside our brains— our thoughts, memories, and feelings— that defines our individual identities.

> John Locke used invisible ink to write risqué letters to his many lady friends.

Continuity of existence

It appears that what makes us who we are depends on our minds, rather than our bodies. Yet we change psychologically as

> **BECAUSE OF THE UNBROKEN NATURE OF THE FLUX BY WHICH MATTER DECAYS AND IS REPLACED, HE IS ALWAYS THE SAME MAN.**
> THOMAS HOBBES

> **AS FAR AS THIS CONSCIOUSNESS CAN BE EXTENDED BACKWARDS TO ANY PAST ACTION OR THOUGHT, SO FAR REACHES THE IDENTITY OF THAT PERSON.**
> JOHN LOCKE

well as physically as we go through life, and we think and feel differently at various stages in life. Our ideas and opinions as a young person may be totally at odds with the beliefs we will have as an older person. We not only feel differently, but are viewed as different by other people. When you meet someone you haven't seen for a long time, he or she may have very different ideas from those of the person you remember, yet is recognizably the same— he or she has retained the same identity. John Locke suggested that just as we have a single continuous life as a physical organism, our minds also have a continuous existence. Personal identity involves continuity of consciousness, which he thought was rooted in memory.

See also: 76–77

THE TELEPORTER

In science fiction, a teleporter can "beam" someone from one place to another. Perhaps, though, the machine doesn't actually transport the person, but makes an identical copy in another place, and destroys the original. The new person is exactly the same, and even thinks he is the original, but obviously isn't. And if by accident the original isn't destroyed, both would believe they have the same identity.

THOMAS HOBBES

1588–1679

Thomas Hobbes was 16 when his father, the vicar of Westport Church in Wiltshire, England, deserted his family after fighting with another vicar on the church steps. The teenage Thomas relied on his uncle, a glove maker, for support as he earned a classics degree at Oxford University. Soon after, he became a tutor to young nobles such as Charles II, the future king of England, Scotland, and Ireland.

ESCAPING WAR

Hobbes traveled widely in Europe with those he tutored, meeting both the astronomer Galileo Galilei and René Descartes. In 1640, when civil war loomed in England, the royalist Hobbes fled to France. During his 11 years there, he published *De Cive* (1642) about the church and state, and completed his highly influential work on society, *Leviathan* (1651).

"SOLITARY, POOR, NASTY, BRUTISH, AND SHORT"

Hobbes's bleak description (above) of a person's life without society stems from his view that people are chiefly selfish beings driven by fear of death and hope of personal gain. Without society, people would enter a "state of nature" where only short-term personal goals mattered, at the expense of cooperation and long-term plans.

A SOCIAL CONTRACT

To escape the state of nature, Hobbes envisioned people forging a social contract: giving up some of their personal freedoms in return for others doing the same, for the sake of security and cooperation. This idea—ceding rights in exchange for the protection of any remaining rights—gained interest, especially in Europe, where Hobbes was held in high regard.

> " **Where men build on false grounds**, the more they build, the **greater is the ruin**. "

"COVENANTS, WITHOUT THE SWORD, ARE BUT WORDS"

Hobbes argued that a social contract would work only if backed by an external form of power that forced people to comply. He used a Leviathan (a mythical sea monster) to represent the power of the state, which he concluded must be an absolute monarchy: A single ruler offered the least competition and friction between different factions of society.

In 1666, *Leviathan* was included on a list of books by the English parliament to be investigated on the charge of atheism. Fearful of arrest, Hobbes burned many of his papers.

Can COMPUTERS

COMPUTER SCIENCE HAS ADVANCED SO MUCH THAT TODAY WE HAVE MACHINES THAT CAN BE PROGRAMMED TO DO ALL KINDS OF TASKS, OFTEN MORE EFFICIENTLY THAN HUMANS. SOME MIMIC THE ACTIVITY OF THE HUMAN BRAIN, AND APPEAR TO BE "THINKING" AND MAKING DECISIONS. ALTHOUGH THEY SHOW SOME KIND OF INTELLIGENCE, MOST OF US INSTINCTIVELY FEEL THAT NO MATTER HOW ADVANCED THE TECHNOLOGY, MACHINES WILL NEVER BE ABLE TO THINK IN THE SAME WAY AS US.

The brain is a soft machine

The idea of "artificial intelligence" emerged from the development of computer science in the second half of the 20th century, at around the same time as advances in neuroscience were providing an insight into the workings of the human brain. The two sciences developed side by side, and each borrowed ideas from the other. New imaging technology revealed the electrochemical activity in our brains that accompanies our thought processes, and computer scientists attempted to make machines that operated in a similar way. If a brain is simply a physical object—a "soft machine"—but is capable of thinking through internal electrical impulses, perhaps eventually a machine could be made to do the same. The field of artificial intelligence has helped produce computers that are not simply "number crunchers," but that mimic our thought processes, even introducing concepts such as "fuzzy logic," so that computers are capable of such complex tasks as recognizing faces and playing chess.

> Alan Turing is famous for his work as a British code breaker during world war II.

> **A COMPUTER WOULD DESERVE TO BE CALLED INTELLIGENT IF IT COULD DECEIVE A HUMAN INTO BELIEVING THAT IT WAS HUMAN.**
> ALAN TURING

The Turing test

In some tasks, these computers achieve results that are indistinguishable from those of humans—often better—and even seem to be able to make decisions. It appears that they have a kind of intelligence, or a form of thought. Alan Turing, a pioneer of computer science, suggested a simple test to show whether a machine is in fact showing intelligence. A computer and a human are both asked a series of written questions, and give written replies. An impartial judge

> **THE PROGRAMMED COMPUTER UNDERSTANDS WHAT THE CAR AND THE ADDING MACHINE UNDERSTAND, NAMELY, EXACTLY NOTHING.**
> JOHN SEARLE

THE CHINESE ROOM

John Searle devised a thought experiment that challenges the validity of the Turing test. A person with no knowledge of Chinese is put into a room with instructions in English of how to respond to a set of Chinese symbols with another set. Chinese people outside can see questions in Chinese going into the room and sensible Chinese answers coming out. They wrongly assume the person in the room is participating in a conversation in Chinese.

think?

I THINK I AM AS INTELLIGENT AS YOU ARE.

See also: 76–77, 78–79

examines the replies, and if he or she cannot tell the difference, the computer has shown it is capable of thinking. John Searle later questioned whether Turing's test really works (see The Chinese room, below left). Today's computers are certainly able to mimic a great deal of human behavior, but it seems we are still a long way from the almost perfectly human androids of science-fiction films such as *Blade Runner*.

Mindless machines

Even if there were an ideal computer that behaved in a way completely indistinguishable from a human, many of us intuitively feel that it would not really have thoughts and feelings. It might give the impression that it has intelligence, and that it thinks and feels, but would it really have this sort of inner life? Or would it merely be simulating mental life? A computer that simulates a hurricane does not really contain a hurricane. So why suppose a computer that simulates thoughts and feelings has real thoughts and feelings? But if no such physical machine can have an inner mental life, how is it that we are able to have such an inner life, given that we appear ultimately to be biological machines? Does it really matter what kind of stuff you are made from?

Faking it ➋
A computer may give the impression that it has intelligence and is thinking in the same way as we do, but perhaps it is not conscious of doing so because machines do not have minds.

Can science explain

JUST AS THE NATURAL SCIENCES EVOLVED FROM PHILOSOPHICAL INQUIRY INTO THE WORLD AROUND US, PSYCHOLOGY AND NEUROSCIENCE DEVELOPED TO HELP US ANSWER PHILOSOPHICAL QUESTIONS ABOUT THE MIND AND THE BRAIN. BUT PERHAPS NOT ALL THE WORKINGS OF OUR MINDS CAN BE SCIENTIFICALLY EXPLAINED.

> OUR BEST **SCIENTIFIC THEORY** ABOUT THE **MIND** IS BETTER THAN PHILOSOPHICAL EMPIRICISM; BUT, IN ALL SORTS OF WAYS, IT'S STILL **NOT VERY GOOD.**
>
> JERRY FODOR

Ancient egyptians didn't value the brain—they believed that the heart was the source of wisdom.

Mind and behavior

Despite its roots in the questions posed by the philosophy of mind, psychology has attempted to find explanations of the way our minds work from a rather different perspective. In place of what psychologists regarded as speculation, they have proposed a number of theories based on scientific observation. For example, behaviorist psychologists examined how we acquire knowledge (a major part of philosophical epistemology) by examining the behavior of animals and humans as they learned things, and by conducting experiments designed to test their theories. Later, cognitive psychologists devised experimental methods to examine how brains store information in memory, and how we perceive things by processing information from our senses. Psychology has also examined other aspects of the workings of our minds, such as intelligence, personality, and emotions, to give scientific explanations of how and why we think and behave the way we do.

How the brain works

Meanwhile, neuroscience has looked at the physical processes of the brain and nervous system. Neuroscientists have learned how information from our sense organs is transmitted to and from our brains as electrochemical signals via our nervous systems, and how the brain processes that information. Using modern imaging methods, they have even been able to see the electrical activity in the brain when we process information from our senses, and during mental processes such as thinking, decision making, remembering, or using language. Although neuroscience has gone a long way toward explaining the workings of our brains, it can only show us what is happening physically when we experience something, which is not, it seems, the same as our subjective conscious experience.

A NEW SCIENCE

Psychology did not appear as a science until the late 19th century. In American universities, psychologists emerged from within the departments of philosophy, while in Europe, experimental psychology was at first considered a branch of physiology. Psychology soon became a new discipline in its own right, the science of mind and behavior—a bridge between philosophy and physiology.

how our MINDS WORK?

Beyond the reach of science?

Neuroscience has provided us with knowledge of the "hardware" of our minds (the physical workings of the brain and nervous system), and psychology has told us much about the "software" (the way our minds process information). These sciences are beginning to answer some of the questions about how we perceive the world and acquire and store knowledge about it. But will such sciences ever be able to tell us what exactly a mind is, or explain our subjective experiences? Why do we have the kind of conscious experiences we do when certain things happen in our brains? Indeed,

why should such brain events be accompanied by conscious experiences at all? Science may be able to tell us a great deal about how our minds work, but it seems there are some questions about our minds and what goes on in them that are still beyond the scope of science.

The search goes on ➲
Psychologists have studied mental processes, and neuroscientists have seen how the brain works. But science has yet to answer the philosophical conundrum of what the mind is.

CAN SCIENTISTS SHED LIGHT ON THE WORKINGS OF YOUR MIND?

See also: 70–71, 82–83

PERSONAL EXPERIENCE

Questions of consciousness, self-awareness, and identity that philosophers have puzzled over have also become a field of scientific study. Neuroscientists are now able to see the activity in our brains, and identify patterns and connections that may help provide an explanation of our subjective experiences.

Philosophy of mind
IN PRACTICE

WHAT A DIFFERENCE

Philosophical theories about what makes us who we are formed the basis for psychological research into the various aspects of our minds that make each of us unique—such as different types of personality and levels of intelligence, and how we develop and change psychologically throughout our lives.

MENTAL HEALTH

Mental disorders such as depression or anxiety are often treated with the so-called "talking cure" of psychotherapy, and traumas such as bereavement can be overcome through counseling. These techniques have developed from the philosophy of mind, which can also help patients make sense of mental problems.

Eastern philosophy has also influenced modern ideas about the mind. Exercises such as yoga and techniques such as meditation—practiced in India and China for centuries—are being taken up in the West, and many psychologists agree they may help maintain physical and mental well-being.

BODY AND SOUL

ARTIFICIAL INTELLIGENCE

Computers were originally designed to perform purely mechanical "number crunching," but are now capable of much more sophisticated operations. Increasingly, we demand that they "think" like we do, and the science of artificial intelligence is based on philosophical and psychological ideas of how our minds work.

Philosophers have raised fundamental questions about our minds—what they are and how they work—that were later taken up by psychologists. Philosophical ideas about the mind have also found some relevance in the development of technologies such as computer science and robotics.

ANIMAL RIGHTS

It has become clear that consciousness is not unique to humans, and that animals, too, have minds—and may therefore experience things not so differently from us. The knowledge that they are capable of both mental and physical suffering has led to a growing movement pressing for a more ethical treatment of animals.

What is
REASONING?

True or false? PROVE IT...

What is a LOGICAL ARGUMENT?

Are there different kinds of TRUTH?

What makes a GOOD ARGUMENT?

What's LOGIC got to do with science?

Can we TRUST what SCIENCE tells us?

Just use COMMON SENSE!

What can LOGIC tell us?

There must be a LOGICAL explanation

Are REASON and FAITH compatible?

Logic evolved as a branch of philosophy as philosophers provided rational arguments to support their theories. It is the science of constructing and analyzing rational arguments, reaching conclusions from certain premises. There are different forms of logical argument; recognizing these helps us assess the strength of a claim.

Valid argument

This argument has two premises, leading to a conclusion. It is valid because the conclusion "Edward likes honey" follows logically from the premises. And if the premises are true, the conclusion must also be true.

ALL BEARS LIKE HONEY. **EDWARD IS A BEAR.** **THUS, EDWARD LIKES HONEY.**

True or false?

PHILOSOPHERS PLACE GREAT EMPHASIS ON THE USE OF REASON. WHEN THEY PROPOSE A THEORY, THEY TRY TO SUPPORT IT WITH A REASONED ARGUMENT. THEY ALSO LOOK FOR LOGICAL FLAWS IN THE ARGUMENTS SUPPOSEDLY SUPPORTING A THEORY. LOGIC ALLOWS US TO BUILD RATIONAL ARGUMENTS AND ASSESS HOW WELL AN ARGUMENT SUPPORTS A THEORY.

See also: 92–93, 94–95, 98–99

Building a rational argument

Simply saying that we believe something is true is unlikely to convince other people of our opinion. We need to back up the belief by showing how we came to that conclusion and presenting an argument to support it. A good argument will show how we moved from one idea to another in a logical way. It should start with statements that are accepted as true—the premises—and infer a conclusion. In order to establish that the conclusion of an argument is true, the premises must be true and the argument logically sound. Logic provides us with a method of assessing whether our inferences are good or bad, and some arguments are stronger than others.

Getting at the truth

Logic helps us to analyze an argument—to see its structure, or logical form. We can then assess whether or not the conclusion follows from the premises. An argument is said to be valid when we can deduce (work out) the conclusion from the premises. Such an argument is known as a deductive argument. In a deductive

RUSSELL'S TEAPOT

Some people, especially those with deeply held religious or political beliefs, don't think they should have to prove their claims; they feel it is up to others to disprove them. In reply to this, Bertrand Russell proposed that there is a teapot orbiting the sun, too small to be detected from Earth. No one can prove him wrong, but this does not mean we should accept his theory.

⊙ Invalid argument
This argument is invalid because the conclusion "Some philosophers are bears" does not follow logically from the argument's two premises. Even if the premises of an invalid argument are true, the conclusion might not be.

ALL BEARS LIKE HONEY.   SOME PHILOSOPHERS LIKE HONEY.   THUS, SOME PHILOSOPHERS ARE BEARS.

PROVE IT...

argument, *if* the premises are true, the conclusion must also be true. But being able to deduce the conclusion from the premises is not enough to prove that the conclusion is true; it also depends on the content of the argument. For example, we can start with the premises "All philosophers are human" and "Aristotle is a philosopher," and move to the conclusion "Aristotle is human." The argument is convincing because it has a sound logical form and the conclusion follows from the two premises. But what if we instead said, "All philosophers are intelligent. Aristotle is a philosopher. Therefore, Aristotle is intelligent"? Like the first example, this argument has two premises leading to a conclusion, but the premise "All philosophers are intelligent" may or may not be true. We need some evidence or another argument to establish its truth.

Degrees of reasonableness
If we can establish that the premises of an argument are very probably all true, and we know that the argument is valid, then we can know that the conclusion is

> A VERY GREAT DEAL MORE **TRUTH** CAN BECOME **KNOWN** THAN CAN BE **PROVEN**.
> RICHARD FEYNMAN

most likely true, too. But sometimes the premises of an argument, although true, do not give us enough information to prove whether or not the conclusion is true. For example, I know that *most* guitarists are right-handed, and that Jim is a guitarist, and this gives me some justification for believing that Jim is likely to be right-handed. Although it is possible to prove that some things are true if the premises are true and the argument is valid, not all arguments are so black and white. There are degrees of reasonableness of belief. As a result, many philosophical arguments set out simply to provide a reasonable justification for an idea—a theory, rather than a proof.

Aristotle loved to argue—he came up with the first system of logic in western philosophy as a result.

What is a **LOGICAL**

RATIONAL ARGUMENTS CAN TAKE MANY FORMS, BUT ALL MOVE IN STEPS FROM PREMISES TO A CONCLUSION. PHILOSOPHERS HAVE USED INCREASINGLY COMPLEX FORMS OF ARGUMENT TO PRESENT AND JUSTIFY THEIR IDEAS, AND THE LOGIC THAT UNDERPINS THESE ARGUMENTS HAS BECOME MORE SOPHISTICATED, DEVELOPING INTO A BRANCH OF PHILOSOPHY WITH CONNECTIONS TO MATH.

> Gottlob Frege was a pioneer of logic, but his work received little recognition in his lifetime.

Aristotle's system

The first philosophers in ancient Greece proposed ideas about the world by using reason, and justification for their beliefs was argued in debate with other thinkers. By the time of Socrates, this was a well-established way of presenting theories. Socrates developed a method, known as the dialectic, of pursuing truth by discussing ideas with people with differing views. A major part of his technique was to show the contradictions inherent in those people's beliefs. But it was Aristotle who devised a system of presenting an argument in a logical form—the syllogism. Logical arguments, he said, consist of two premises leading to a conclusion. Each step of the argument is a statement, or proposition, in a particular form, such as "All X are Y," "Some X are Y," "No X are Y," or "Some X are not Y." Aristotle then classified the various combinations of these statements, identifying which of them provided good or bad conclusions.

> IT REALLY IS WORTH THE TROUBLE TO INVENT A NEW **SYMBOL** IF IT HELPS US REMOVE MANY **LOGICAL** DIFFICULTIES.
>
> GOTTLOB FREGE

Deduction and induction

A famous example of a syllogism is "All men are mortal. Socrates is a man. Therefore, Socrates is mortal." Here, the conclusion "Socrates is mortal" is logically entailed by the universal premise "All men are mortal," in combination with the premise "Socrates is a man." Deductive arguments such as this one are valid if the conclusion follows from the premises, and invalid if it doesn't. But there is another form of argument, called induction, in which a general rule is often inferred from particular premises. For example, we infer that all fish have gills from the particular instances of fish that we have observed, but that conclusion may be false—there may be (and, in fact, are) some fish that have lungs instead of gills. In an inductive argument, the conclusion does not necessarily follow from its premises. Inductive arguments are not supposed to be valid. The premises are meant to support, but not logically guarantee the truth of, their conclusions.

Mathematical logic

Aristotle's method of analyzing an argument as a three-step syllogism remained the basis for logic until the end of the 19th century, but it had its limitations as a means of analyzing arguments. German mathematician Gottlob Frege revolutionized the way that philosophical arguments could be

SYMBOLIC LOGIC

When Gottlob Frege showed the connection between logic and math, he also suggested a system of notation to express logical statements, using symbols similar to the signs used in math. In this way, a proposition can be presented in a logical form, and analyzed according to the rules of logic, so that the argument can be tested in a similar way to a mathematical proof.

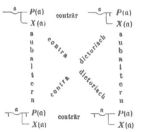

ARGUMENT?

assessed. Previously, it had been thought that logic was derived from the way we think, but Frege demonstrated that, like math, it is based on a set of objective rules. He introduced a system of notation (see Symbolic logic, below left) to present arguments in a logical form. This ironed out the ambiguities of philosophical arguments presented verbally, allowing philosophers to analyze logical propositions in the same way that mathematicians analyze mathematical statements. It also provided a new framework for logic, making it a much more powerful tool, and paving the way for a more analytical form of philosophy in the 20th century.

See also: 90–91, 98–99, 108–109

Contrary
The statements "All bears like honey" and "No bears like honey" are contrary propositions. They are opposites, since they can't both be true at the same time, but it is possible that they are both false—that some bears like honey and some don't.

NO BEARS LIKE HONEY.

ALL BEARS LIKE HONEY.

Contradictory
The propositions at opposite corners of the square contradict one another—if one is true, the other must be false. If all bears like honey, it can't be true that some don't, and vice versa. But the propositions on this and the opposite side are not contradictory in this way.

THERE ARE FOUR BASIC FORMS OF PROPOSITIONS.

The square of opposition
Philosophers using Aristotle's system of syllogisms devised a diagram presenting the four basic forms of propositions. It shows how some propositions are opposed, in that if one is true, the other can't be.

SOME BEARS LIKE HONEY.

Subcontrary
The propositions along the bottom of the square are a different kind of opposite. They do not contradict each other, and both can be true at the same time—some bears like honey, but there are others that don't.

SOME BEARS DON'T LIKE HONEY.

Are there different kinds of **TRUTH**?

PHILOSOPHICAL ARGUMENTS ARE LARGELY CONCERNED WITH ESTABLISHING THE TRUTH OF AN IDEA OR PROPOSITION. BUT THERE ARE DIFFERENT WAYS OF ESTABLISHING WHETHER A STATEMENT IS TRUE OR FALSE. SOMETIMES, WE CAN USE REASON AND LOGIC ALONE TO SHOW THAT SOMETHING IS TRUE, WHILE AT OTHER TIMES WE MUST OBSERVE THE WORLD AROUND US.

> **THERE ARE TWO KINDS OF TRUTHS: TRUTHS OF REASONING AND TRUTHS OF FACT.**
>
> GOTTFRIED LEIBNIZ

Two types of truths

The philosopher and mathematician Gottfried Leibniz believed that there is more than one type of truth. He identified two different kinds of statements, which he supposed to be true in different ways. The first he called a "truth of reasoning," and explained that it can be verified by reason alone. For example, the statement "All tomcats are male" is such a truth because the definition of *tomcat* is "a male cat."

In fact, this example is what philosophers call an analytic truth—it is true because of its meaning. But what about a statement such as "Socrates is in the next room"? We can only tell if this statement is true by looking in the next room to see if Socrates is there. This is what Leibniz called a "truth of fact," rather than a truth of reasoning. Statements like this that cannot be true because of their meaning alone are known as synthetic, as opposed to analytic, truths.

See also: 102–103

Denying truths without contradiction

According to Leibniz, truths of reasoning cannot be denied without contradiction. We cannot deny a truth of reasoning such as "All squares have four sides" and assert, "There is a square without four sides," without contradicting ourselves. This would be the same as saying there is something four-sided that does not have four sides. The fact that all squares have four sides is also what is known as a necessary truth—it is true in all circumstances and in all possible worlds. On the other hand, a truth of fact such as "Abraham Lincoln was American" could be contradicted. It happens to be the case that Lincoln was born in the United States, but circumstances might have been different—he might have been born elsewhere. Because it depends on whether something actually is the case or not, such a truth is known as a contingent truth.

Hume's fork

The distinction between truths of reasoning and truths of fact is particularly

TRUTHS ARE EITHER...

TRUTHS OF REASONING
THE ROAD OF REASONING ALONE WILL BRING YOU NO KNOWLEDGE OF THE WORLD—JUST TRIVIAL TRUTHS, SUCH AS THE FACT THAT A SQUARE HAS FOUR SIDES.

... RELATIONS OF IDEAS

important in the philosophy of David Hume. He regarded statements as concerning either "relations of ideas" or "matters of fact," and likened these categories to two different directions after a fork in a road. Hume argued that true statements about relations of ideas can be known by reason alone, and will be necessary truths, but that they are trivial (like the statement that squares have four sides) and give us no knowledge about the world. True statements concerning matters of fact, on the other hand, really can provide us with information about the world—but we need to observe the world to find out if they are true. Hume thought that we cannot cross from one fork of the road to the other— we can't gain knowledge of real matters of fact by relying on reason alone.

German company Bahlsen produces the "Leibniz" biscuit, named after the philosopher Gottfried Leibniz.

... OR MATTERS OF FACT.

MATH AND SCIENCE
The difference between necessary and contingent truths reflects the fundamental difference between math and the natural sciences. Mathematical truths appear to be knowable by reason alone—they are necessary truths. However, scientific discoveries, such as the fact that water boils at 212°F (100°C) at 1 atmosphere, are contingent truths—they rely on observation, and, unlike mathematical truths, are not indisputable.

TRUTHS OF FACT
ALTERNATIVELY, TAKE THE EMPIRICAL ROAD. ACCORDING TO DAVID HUME, ONLY THIS ROUTE CAN LEAD TO REAL KNOWLEDGE ABOUT THE WORLD.

ARISTOTLE

384–322 BCE

Aristotle was initially expected to follow in the footsteps of his father, Nicomachus, who was the physician to Amyntas III, king of Macedonia. Instead, he studied philosophy in Athens, traveled to Turkey and Lesbos to study marine life, and in 343 BCE became the tutor of 13-year-old Alexander the Great, teaching him for eight years. Returning to Athens, Aristotle was prolific, writing as many as 200 works, of which about 30 survive.

Aristotle's science had major flaws, such as his assertions that females of all species had fewer teeth than males, and that human thought came not from the brain, but from an area around the heart.

PLATO'S PUPIL

Aristotle was 17 when he was sent to study at Plato's Academy in Athens. He spent 20 years with Plato, who called him "the mind of the school." Aristotle developed his own theories in opposition to his tutor, rejecting Plato's theory of forms and insisting that universal qualities are found in things themselves. Aristotle left Athens shortly after Plato died in 347 BCE.

A SCHOOL OF HIS OWN

Aristotle returned to Athens in 335 BCE and founded his own school at the Lyceum gymnasium just outside the city. He stocked it with a substantial library of scrolls (possibly funded by Alexander the Great) and formed one of the very first zoos using gifts of exotic animals. Students at the school elected a new leader or representative every 10 days.

SOCRATES IS MORTAL

Aristotle believed that the use of reason was the highest form of endeavor and that logic was the tool by which people came to know things. His pioneering system of logic featured syllogisms—conclusions made from two premises. For example, if the premises "All men are mortal" and "Socrates is a man" are accepted, then one can deduce "Therefore, Socrates is mortal."

"**Wisdom** must be intuitive reason combined with **scientific knowledge**."

ANIMAL LOGIC

Aristotle's scientific work ranged from astronomy to zoology. He was the first person to differentiate whales and dolphins from fish, and he dissected hundreds of creatures in an effort to understand how they worked. Using logic, he classified organisms into a pioneering *Scala Naturae* or "Chain of Being"—a huge classification system that was influential for 2,000 years.

What makes a GOOD ARGUMENT?

TO BE COGENT (LOGICAL AND CONVINCING), AN ARGUMENT MUST BE BASED ON PREMISES THAT ARE TRUE, OR AT LEAST REASONABLE, AND PROVIDE SUPPORT FOR THE CONCLUSION. AN ARGUMENT CAN BE PRESENTED IN SEVERAL DIFFERENT WAYS, AND THE LOGICAL FORM IT TAKES DETERMINES WHETHER IT IS RIGHT TO INFER THE CONCLUSION FROM THE PREMISES.

YOU CAN'T BEAT A VALID ARGUMENT...

Artist M. C. Escher used perspective to create visual paradoxes in his art, such as staircases that appear never-ending.

Analyzing an argument

For centuries, the principal method of analyzing an argument was based on Aristotle's model of the syllogism. According to this, an argument consists of two premises and a conclusion, and to constitute a good argument, it had to satisfy certain criteria. Each statement within the argument is made up of two terms, which may be universal (such as "all X are Y" or "no X are Y") or particular (such as "some X are Y" or "some X are not Y"). Various combinations of these types of statements give, in total, a possible 256 different forms of syllogisms, and these have been classified according to whether or not the conclusion can be inferred from the premises. Only some forms are valid deductive arguments, in which a particular conclusion follows from a universal premise, and if the premises are true, the conclusion must also be true. Other forms include examples of errors of reasoning, which are known as fallacies, or examples of arguments such as induction, in which the premises support, but do not logically guarantee the truth of, the conclusion.

> THERE ARE **NO WHOLE TRUTHS;** ALL TRUTHS ARE **HALF-TRUTHS.** IT IS TRYING TO TREAT THEM AS WHOLE TRUTHS THAT PLAYS THE DEVIL.
>
> ALFRED NORTH WHITEHEAD

The problem of half-truths

Logic based on Aristotle's analysis of arguments had its shortcomings, however. While it quite easily showed whether a deductive argument was valid or not, it was not an adequate system for assessing the strength of a conclusion that could be neither proved nor disproved. The mathematical logic introduced by Gottlob Frege in the 19th century helped provide a more sophisticated model for determining the strength of logical arguments. Yet the problem remained that arguments depended on the idea that something is either true or false, when in fact there are such things as "half-truths." Recently, a system of "fuzzy logic" has been established to give a continuum between true (given a value of 1) and false (given a value of 0), so that something that is a half-truth could be expressed by a value of 0.5, a pretty likely probability by 0.9, and a remote possibility by 0.1.

IT CAN'T BE TRUE!

Epimenides of Crete is credited with producing the famous paradox "All Cretans are liars." In saying this, he admits that he himself doesn't tell the truth. The statement itself is simple enough, but because it is self-contradictory, it leads us back to the beginning: If it's true, then he's lying, but if he's lying, it can't be true.

Puzzling paradoxes

Even a seemingly sound argument, based on apparently true premises, can lead to a conclusion that is obviously wrong or contradictory—a paradox. It is often difficult to see if this is due simply to faulty reasoning, or to false, ambiguous, or even contradictory premises. One of the most famous paradoxes was devised by Zeno of Elea, who presents a compelling argument that Achilles can never catch up with a tortoise if he gives it a head start in a race (see illustration, left). Using the tools of traditional logic, philosophers found it difficult to fault his reasoning. And that's the trouble with paradoxes— they are apparently logically sound, but lead to absurd conclusions. Even sophisticated modern mathematical techniques haven't yet come up with a simple solution to Zeno's puzzle.

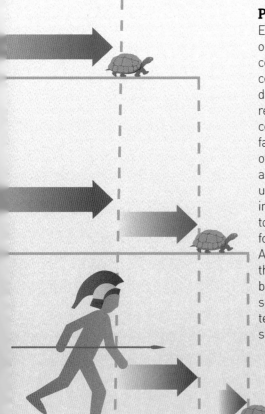

◕ Achilles and the tortoise

In Zeno of Elea's paradox, Achilles will never succeed in overtaking the tortoise because by the time he reaches the tortoise's current position, the tortoise will already have moved on.

See also: 90–91, 92–93, 102–103

What's **LOGIC** got to do with science?

THE NATURAL SCIENCES ARE BASED ON OBSERVATION AND EXPERIMENT, UNLIKE MATH, WHICH IS BASED ON LOGICAL REASONING. BUT IN TRYING TO UNDERSTAND THE THINGS THEY OBSERVE, SCIENTISTS HAVE DEVELOPED METHODS OF EXAMINING THEM AND PRESENTING THE EVIDENCE TO JUSTIFY THEIR THEORIES IN A LOGICAL FASHION.

Looking for rules

Often considered the originator of the scientific approach, Aristotle was systematic in every aspect of his work. In addition to being the first to analyze and classify logical arguments, and methodically organize aspects of his philosophy, he was an enthusiastic naturalist, and arranged his observations of the natural world just as methodically. He aimed to classify all living things, and approached the task in a logical way, grouping together plants and animals according to their characteristics. He observed, for example, that all the fish he had seen had scales, and concluded that this characteristic distinguished fish from other marine animals. In this way, he built up a set of general rules from his observations.

SCIENTISTS TACKLE PROBLEMS IN A LOGICAL WAY.

IF A MAN WILL BE CONTENT TO BEGIN WITH **DOUBTS**, HE SHALL END IN **CERTAINTIES.**

FRANCIS BACON

A scientific method

Aristotle's method was simple, but it established the principle of observing and then analyzing the data resulting from those observations. This could then be used as evidence to support an idea, or hypothesis. This principle was later adopted by Islamic scientists and philosophers, who not only observed things as they occurred in the natural world, but also in experiments. This, in turn, led to a more systematic approach—a truly scientific method—proposed by English philosopher Francis Bacon. Bacon's method follows a logical sequence of steps: observation,

MAKE AN OBSERVATION
HERE, A SCIENTIST MIGHT OBSERVE THAT AN OBJECT, POSSIBLY A VASE, IS BROKEN, AND THAT IT WAS MADE UP OF THREE DIFFERENT COLORS.

FORM A HYPOTHESIS
THE SCIENTIST WOULD THEN TRY TO EXPLAIN HOW THE OBJECT SHOULD LOOK. PERHAPS THE PIECES FIT TOGETHER IN THREE COLORED BANDS?

> **francis Bacon died of pneumonia, contracted while stuffing snow into a chicken as an experiment in refrigeration.**

forming a hypothesis to explain a certain phenomenon, and testing that hypothesis with experiments designed to produce the expected results. In this scientific method, unlike other forms of inquiry, investigators don't simply infer a general rule from observed instances of a phenomenon. Instead, they use these observations to predict that the same thing will happen in similar circumstances—the hypothesis. They then see if this is actually the case by reproducing the circumstances in experiments. It is the results of these experiments that either support or disprove a theory.

CLEVER COMPUTERS

The first computers did basic arithmetical tasks, programmed with simple mathematical rules. To get them to do more complex things, it is necessary to convert those tasks into a logical progression of steps, each one in a logical form that the computer can "understand." New forms of mathematical logic were crucial in transforming computers from simple calculating devices into machines capable of showing artificial intelligence.

Testing results

Like Aristotle's method of observing particular instances and inferring a general rule, the scientific method is a form of inductive reasoning. As such, it cannot prove that a theory is true. But the more instances that are observed, the stronger the evidence

is for a theory, and the process of critical experimentation offers even stronger evidence. The results of one experiment can be tested by conducting another experiment to see if those results are replicated. And, to ensure that the results are as reliable and objective as possible, sophisticated techniques of experimentation, measurement, and analysis of data have been devised. For example, in medicine, a treatment may be tested by giving it to a number of patients at the same time as control groups are given either a placebo (a substance with no therapeutic effect) or no treatment at all. The results from each group are then compared, and the effectiveness of the treatment can be measured statistically. In this way, both logic and math play an important role in the scientific method.

See also: 92–93, 102–103

See also: 92–93, 102–103

PERFORM AN EXPERIMENT
THE NEXT STAGE IS TO TEST THE HYPOTHESIS BY PERFORMING AN EXPERIMENT—SEEING IF THE PIECES FIT TOGETHER AS SUPPOSED.

SEE THE RESULTS
LASTLY, THE SCIENTIST WILL LOOK AT WHETHER OR NOT THE RESULTS SUPPORT THE HYPOTHESIS. THE REPAIRED VASE SHOWS THAT THEY DO.

ALL SWANS ARE WHITE...

Can we **TRUST** what

WE LIVE IN A WORLD DOMINATED BY THE PRODUCTS OF SCIENCE, FROM COMPUTERS TO GENETICALLY MODIFIED CROPS. SCIENCE HAS ALSO GONE A LONG WAY TOWARD EXPLAINING HOW THE UNIVERSE WORKS. WE TEND TO ACCEPT THESE EXPLANATIONS AS TRUE, BUT SOME PHILOSOPHERS HAVE ARGUED THAT WE HAVE NO LOGICAL BASIS FOR BELIEVING THEM.

OUR PAST EXPERIENCE CAN BE A PROOF OF NOTHING FOR THE FUTURE.
DAVID HUME

The problem of induction

Scientific theories can only be based on the evidence available, so observations of particular instances are used to support general conclusions about what might happen in the future or everywhere in the universe. This is inductive reasoning, which scientists rely on in trying to tell us something about the world. For example, I might conclude that when I let go of a ball, it will fall to the ground because every time I have dropped a ball, it has fallen, or infer that since I have seen the sun rise every morning, it will do so again tomorrow and every day afterward. But what grounds do I have for believing this? David Hume argued that our dependence on inductive reasoning is wholly unjustified. We have no more reason to suppose

All of science's top achievements, from machines to space travel, have relied on induction.

the sun will rise tomorrow than we have to suppose it will not. The problem of induction, he explained, is that it relies on the assumption that everything in the universe follows an unchanging pattern, and that the future will resemble the past. But this assumption is itself based on inductive reasoning—we assume that nature is uniform because our limited experience tells us that it is so. Similarly, just because in our experience one event has invariably followed another, does not mean that the first event caused the second. If two clocks are set a few seconds apart, one always chimes after the other, but not because of it. Science, Hume said, is a matter of custom and habit, not reasoning— we cannot help but believe these things. It may seem ridiculous to suggest that the sun is just as likely *not* to rise tomorrow as it is to rise, but philosophers have struggled to find fault with Hume's argument.

... OR ARE THEY?

⬆ Dubious logic
The conclusion "All swans are white" isn't logically guaranteed to be true, no matter how many white swans you see, but a single sighting of a black swan establishes it as false.

SCIENCE tells us?

Not all cats have tails

The problem of induction called into doubt how much we can trust scientific theories, and remained unresolved until Karl Popper suggested a different approach in the mid-20th century. Popper agreed that several observed instances can't confirm a general principle, but pointed out that a single negative instance can falsify that theory. No matter how many positive sightings I make of cats with tails, I cannot be certain of the truth of the theory "All cats have tails"—but just one sighting of a cat with no tail shows it is false. According to Popper, theories are scientific only if they are falsifiable (capable of being shown to be false by observation or experiment).

But induction works!

Can we show that it is reasonable to trust inductive reasoning by showing that it works? After all, scientists have sent people to the moon by relying on inductive arguments. Don't such scientific triumphs show that we are justified in trusting these

> **HUME WAS PERFECTLY RIGHT IN POINTING OUT THAT INDUCTION CANNOT BE LOGICALLY JUSTIFIED.**
> **KARL POPPER**

arguments? Unfortunately, this argument is itself an inductive argument. It says that induction has worked up to now, so it will probably work tomorrow.

See also: 26–27, 92–93, 100–101

THE GAMBLER'S FALLACY

If you toss a perfect coin, there's a 50-50 chance that it will come up heads. This means that if it is tossed 100 times, the chances are that it will be heads 50 times. But it is easy to fall into the trap of believing that if the coin has come up tails 99 times in a row, it's much more likely to be heads next time. This is a fallacy, since the probability of it coming up heads remains 50-50 with each toss.

Just use COMMON SENSE!

LOGIC OFTEN SEEMS VERY ABSTRACT, WITH LITTLE CONNECTION TO THE WORLD WE LIVE IN. WE CAN'T USE IT TO DETERMINE IF SCIENTIFIC THEORIES ARE TRUE, AND EVEN SOUND LOGICAL ARGUMENTS CAN LEAD TO PARADOXES THAT DEFY COMMON SENSE. SO PERHAPS THERE IS A PLACE FOR COMMON SENSE, AS WELL AS LOGIC, IN JUSTIFYING OUR BELIEFS.

See also: 26–27, 98–99, 100–101, 102–103

Common sense and intuition

To some extent, logic can be regarded as "common sense" in a highly organized form. Many of the inferences that we make without consciously analyzing them are the same as those of a logical argument, and we often recognize when a conclusion does or does not follow from a statement, without referring to the rules of logic. Sometimes, however, our common sense can let us down. For many early astronomers, for example, common sense seemed to dictate that the earth was flat and that the sun moved across the earth's sky. And, at times, what seems to be common sense is no more than a gut feeling, or intuition, which is a poor justification for a belief. But while a good argument needs to be based on logic, common sense and intuition also play a part. In the case of paradoxes (when apparently sound premises or statements lead to an absurd conclusion), for instance, we intuitively feel that something is wrong. Common sense also tells us that the reasoning is faulty, so we can then use logic to examine the argument more carefully.

> The first person known to have used the term *common sense* is Aristotle, in the context of animals' minds.

Simple is best

William of Ockham, a medieval monk and philosopher, advocated a particular kind of common sense when deciding between competing explanations and arguments. Too often, he felt, philosophers produced elaborate explanations, based on multiple premises, to justify their theories. He said that when we are faced with more than one explanation for something, all things being equal, the simpler explanation is more likely to be correct. This principle is known as Ockham's (or Occam's) razor, as it "shaves off" all unnecessary assumptions. David Hume adopted

SLAVE OF THE PASSIONS

While David Hume advocated basing our reasoning on experience, he also realized that our judgments and decisions tend to be based more on our feelings than on rational thinking. We are more likely to use our intellect to justify what our emotions and instinctive drives are telling us, or, as he put it: "Reason is the slave of the passions."

Occam's razor ➔

William of Ockham felt that philosophers tended to overcomplicate things. He argued that when multiple explanations of equal weight are offered, the simplest explanation is likely to be the most valid.

a similar approach in his criticism of René Descartes and the rationalist philosophers, asking why it was necessary to propose the existence of an immaterial world to justify their theories.

Let custom be the guide

Instead, Hume and the other empiricist philosophers aimed to put their philosophy on the same footing as the sciences, by justifying their ideas with evidence from the world around them. And, having shown that there is no logical justification for the inductive reasoning of science (see pages 102–103), Hume explained that we naturally use custom—or, as he put it, "mental habit"—as a guide. Scientific beliefs cannot be justified, he thought, but we can't help drawing conclusions about the future based on past experience. Here again, common sense has a role. If something happens that appears to defy the general rules, the "laws" of nature or physics we have inferred from our experience, and is reported to be a miracle, our common sense—which is also derived from experience—tells us that it is unlikely to be true. The likelihood that an event contradicting all our experience is miraculous is less than the likelihood that our senses have been deceived, or that reports of the event are false.

SHAVE AWAY UNNECESSARY ASSUMPTIONS

IT IS **POINTLESS** TO DO WITH **MORE** WHAT CAN BE DONE WITH **FEWER.**

WILLIAM OF OCKHAM

LUDWIG WITTGENSTEIN

1889–1951

One of the 20th century's foremost thinkers, Ludwig Wittgenstein was schooled at home in Vienna until he was 14, after which he studied math and engineering. He became obsessed with logic and philosophy, moving to Cambridge, England, to study logic under Bertrand Russell in 1911. The manuscript of his first major work, *Tractatus Logico-Philosophicus*, was kept in his backpack during World War I. Russell received it while Wittgenstein was held prisoner.

THE FAMILY WITTGENSTEIN

Rich from steelmaking, the Wittgensteins were well connected, and composers Gustav Mahler and Johannes Brahms were regular visitors to the family's Vienna home. Ludwig was the youngest of eight children. Tragically, three of his brothers committed suicide. His remaining brother, Paul, was a renowned concert pianist, who, having lost his right arm in World War I, went on to commission many piano pieces for the left hand alone.

WAR SERVICE

Volunteering for the Austrian army when World War I began, Wittgenstein served on ships and in artillery workshops before being posted to the Russian front in 1916. He won a number of medals for bravery in battle, but was captured in Italy and imprisoned until August 1919, nine months after the war had ended.

During World War II, Wittgenstein left Cambridge and worked as a hospital porter in Guy's Hospital, London, and then as a laboratory assistant in Newcastle for a salary of four pounds a week.

LANGUAGE AND LOGIC

In *Tractatus* (1921), Wittgenstein considered the relationship of language to the world and how philosophical problems arise from misunderstandings of the logic of language. He later argued that philosophical problems were generated by linguistic confusion, but supposed such problems could be dissolved by paying close attention to how language is used.

> " The **complexity** of **philosophy** is not a complexity of its subject matter, but of our knotted **understanding**."

THE RELUCTANT PROFESSOR

After working as a village school teacher and gardener, Wittgenstein returned to Cambridge as a lecturer in 1929, becoming a professor in 1939. His lectures were dense and given without notes, while he reclined in a deck chair. He often left promptly, rushing off to the movies to watch his beloved westerns. He even urged students to find a "more useful line of work" than philosophy.

What can LOGIC

ONE OF THE PROBLEMS WE FACE WHEN TRYING TO EVALUATE ARGUMENTS IS THAT THEY ARE NORMALLY PRESENTED IN A VERY ROUGH WAY. IT IS OFTEN NOT CLEAR EXACTLY WHAT THE ARGUMENT IS. SOMETIMES, BEFORE WE CAN ASSESS WHETHER OR NOT AN ARGUMENT'S LOGIC IS SOUND AND ITS PREMISES ARE TRUE, WE NEED TO ANALYZE IT CAREFULLY.

> ## THERE IS MUCH PLEASURE TO BE GAINED FROM USELESS KNOWLEDGE.
> **BERTRAND RUSSELL**

See also: 90–91, 92–93

Ordinary language

Philosophers (as well as politicians, lawyers, and scientists) use arguments to try to justify their explanations. We can use logic to assess the strength of those arguments. However, we do not always speak and write in a way that makes our arguments clear. Often, it helps in philosophy to "translate" what someone is saying into a clearer logical form. Identifying the various premises of an argument and how they relate to its conclusion makes it easier to assess how good the argument really is. Sometimes, even statements that look simple require detailed analysis to determine exactly what they mean. Bertrand Russell believed it was important that philosophers carefully reveal the underlying "logical form" of what is said in ordinary language. To establish the truth of a statement, we must first know its meaning.

A prominent antiwar activist, Russell was imprisoned twice by the British government.

Logical analysis

Russell is perhaps best known for his "theory of descriptions." A description is a phrase of the form "the so-and-so"—such as "the queen of England" or "the planet Earth"—which refers to a particular person or thing (just as names do). We use a description to say something true or false about that person or thing—for example, "The queen of England lives in a palace." The trouble is that some phrases look as though they refer to particular people or things, but in fact don't refer to anything. For instance, the sentence "The king of France is bald" *appears* to make a single claim about something, "the King of France"—namely, that he is bald. But France doesn't have a king, so this phrase refers to no one—it fails as a description (the definition of a description being a phrase that *refers* to something). Russell said that the key to making such phrases meaningful was understanding that rather

LOGICAL SUMS

Between 1910 and 1913, Bertrand Russell (right) and his former teacher Alfred North Whitehead published a three-volume book on logic, *Principia Mathematica*. In it, they set out to show that arithmetic is derived from the basic principles of logic, and that math is, in fact, simply a branch of logic.

tell us?

than making a single claim, the sentence contains three distinct claims. To find the sentence's true logical form (and then assess if it is true or false), we must first break it down: (1) there is at least one king of France, and (2) at most one king of France, and (3) if there is such a king, then he is bald. Now, the sentence is meaningful, but false if there is no king of France. Russell's analysis solves the problem of how nonreferring phrases can be used meaningfully to make true or false claims. But philosophers disagree over whether or not he was right.

Seeing nobody

Other expressions, such as *nobody* and *everything*, also fail to refer. Philosophers call these quantifiers. Take this quotation from *Through the Looking-Glass* by Lewis Carroll (who was also a logician and whose work fascinated Russell): "'I see nobody on the road,' said Alice. 'I only wish I had such eyes,' the King remarked in a fretful tone. 'To be able to see Nobody!'" Here, the King treats *nobody* as if it refers to someone, but that's not how it is used. "Frank ran" and "Nobody ran" are sentences that look similar, but *nobody* is not a name in the way *Frank* is. Really, what Alice is saying is that the number of people she can see on the road is zero.

❷ The logic in language

Before we can find out whether the statement "The solid gold mountain is in Tibet" is true or not, it must first be broken down into a logical form to ensure that we understand its meaning.

HOW TO ANALYZE A STATEMENT

THE SOLID GOLD MOUNTAIN IS IN TIBET.

THERE IS AT LEAST ONE SOLID GOLD MOUNTAIN.

THERE IS AT MOST ONE SOLID GOLD MOUNTAIN.

IF IT IS SUCH A MOUNTAIN, THEN IT IS IN TIBET

PHILOSOPHERS HAVE PRESENTED NUMEROUS THEORIES ABOUT THE UNIVERSE AND OUR PLACE IN IT, AND USED LOGICAL ARGUMENTS TO BACK THEM UP. BUT ALTHOUGH WE HAVE LANGUAGE TO DESCRIBE PHYSICAL THINGS, LANGUAGE CAN BE INADEQUATE TO DISCUSS OTHER THINGS, SUCH AS RELIGIOUS BELIEFS, OR CLAIMS ABOUT MORALITY AND ETHICS.

Picturing the world

As several philosophers had done before, Ludwig Wittgenstein set out to see if there are limits to our understanding of the world. The approach he took was to examine the way in which we use language to articulate our thoughts about the world. In trying to understand and explain the world, he said, we describe it using language. Language allows us to "picture" the world. The world has a structure, and the language we use to represent it has the same

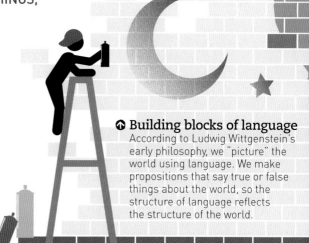

⬆ Building blocks of language
According to Ludwig Wittgenstein's early philosophy, we "picture" the world using language. We make propositions that say true or false things about the world, so the structure of language reflects the structure of the world.

There must be a

structure. We can use names, such as *dog*, to label elements of reality. This gives us the building blocks of language. We can then combine these names in different ways to produce different propositions about, or "pictures" of, the world—for example, "The dog is barking". The propositions will be true or false depending on whether or not the world is as we have "pictured" it (our proposition will be true if the dog is barking, and false if it is not).

The limits of language

For language to have any meaning, though, the propositions must be made up of names that label elements of the world that we have experienced. Wittgenstein argued that meaningful language is restricted to such propositions. He believed

> Ludwig wittgenstein was very secretive about his work, and kept it locked in a safe.

> THE **LIMITS** OF MY **LANGUAGE** ARE THE LIMITS OF MY **WORLD**.
> LUDWiG WiTTGENSTEiN

that claims concerning ethics, morality, metaphysics, and religion are not meaningful propositions. They do not "picture" anything, and so do not succeed in asserting anything. However, he thought that they were still capable of showing us something, including "mystical" things that cannot be put into words.

Private and public language

Wittgenstein later changed his mind about language. He realized that language is, in fact, used in a great variety of ways, and not just to make claims about

LANGUAGE HELPS US BUILD UP A PICTURE OF HOW WE SEE OUR WORLD.

PROPOSITIONS

LOGICAL explanation

the world. This led him to develop a very different philosophy that emphasized the idea that language is like a toolbox: It contains a wide range of expressions that are used in all kinds of different ways. But perhaps the best-known argument from Wittgenstein's later philosophy is his "private language argument." He asserted that we cannot meaningfully attach labels to experiences that are private, or subjective (such as feeling the sensation of pain), because we would have no way of checking if we were applying the label correctly. Therefore, this private language would be meaningless. Wittgenstein thought that there must also be a "public language," in which words acquire their meaning from the way we use them. A word or statement does not mean a specific thing; its meaning depends on the context in which it is used.

In his view, all philosophical problems result from linguistic confusion, caused by how language is actually used. He argued that we don't need solutions to such problems; we need to be shown that there never was a problem in the first place.

See also: 108–109

BEETLE IN A BOX

To demonstrate his ideas of private and public language, Wittgenstein used the analogy that we each have a box with something in it that no one else can see. We call that thing a "beetle." Everyone says they know what a beetle is by looking in his or her own box—but we may all have something different. We all know that when we say "beetle," we mean "what's inside my box," regardless of what each box contains.

Are REASON and

WE SHOULDN'T TRY TO REASON...

THE FIRST PHILOSOPHERS USED REASONING TO TRY TO UNDERSTAND THE WORLD AROUND THEM, OFFERING RATIONAL EXPLANATIONS IN PLACE OF CONVENTIONAL BELIEFS. BUT PHILOSOPHICAL REASONING HAS BEEN USED TO JUSTIFY RELIGIOUS BELIEFS AS WELL AS TO CONTRADICT THEM, AND THERE ARE SOME THINGS THAT REASON ALONE CANNOT EXPLAIN.

> Daoism, confucianism, and Buddhism can be seen as philosophies or religions, as reason and faith play a part in their worldviews.

The immortals

Although the early Greek philosophers sought rational explanations as an alternative to traditional beliefs, this did not appear to threaten their religion. Their idea of religion was very different from our notions of a supreme being: It was taken for granted that immortal gods existed, but their lives were similar to humans', and they did not dictate how humans should behave. Still, few philosophers dared to be openly atheist since it was not a good idea to criticize traditional ideas of the gods. Rather than simply accept such things as a supreme being or an immortal soul as a matter of faith, philosophers such as Plato used reasoning to justify belief in them.

Christianity and Islam

With the growth of Christianity in Europe, attitudes toward rational thought changed dramatically. All aspects of medieval life were dominated by the Church, which expected absolute faith in its doctrines. Theology (the study of God and religious beliefs) took precedence over philosophy, and the legacy of Greek philosophers was viewed with suspicion and often hostility. Slowly, ideas from Plato and Aristotle were accepted, but philosophical reasoning (which was explained as a God-given ability) was largely used to provide rational justifications for articles of faith, such as the existence of God, or heaven and hell. Islam, on the other hand, saw little incompatibility between its beliefs and

FAITH compatible?

... ABOUT FAITH.

Western philosophy. Alongside theology, Islamic scholars studied and refined the work of Greek philosophers, and made great advances in math and science. They implicitly recognized that faith and reason both have a place.

A secular world?

During the Renaissance in Europe, the Church lost much of its power. Religious leaders were replaced with political ones, and societies based their laws on the reasoning of moral philosophy rather than divine commandments. A scientific revolution was also under way, challenging many religious beliefs. The idea grew that rational thought and religious faith could coexist, but were entirely separate. This view has persisted to the present, despite the growth in the 19th century of materialist philosophy, which asserted that only material things can exist, and the emergence of philosophers who argued that there is no place for anything that

can't be explained by reason. Today, most philosophers accept that some things cannot be proven by reason, and that philosophy and science can't answer everything. And even though reasoning, and science in particular, may contradict some of the basic beliefs of religion, there are many scientists and philosophers who have religious faith. However, the danger occurs when reasoning is used to prop up something that has already been accepted on faith, or when faith is used as a substitute for reasoning. When rational and scientific arguments are denied on the strength of religious or political dogma, rational debate can be difficult.

See also: 44–45, 66–67

> DO NOT SEEK TO UNDERSTAND IN ORDER TO BELIEVE, BUT BELIEVE THAT THOU MAYEST UNDERSTAND.
> AUGUSTINE OF HIPPO

FINDING SOLUTIONS

Many jobs involve an element of problem solving or decision making. Before forging ahead, it's important that we think about the task and the options available. By analyzing a problem, we can more easily see the logical consequences, and plan a course of action.

POWER OF PERSUASION

We often have to persuade other people to accept our point of view and convince them of our ideas. This might be in a formal debate or presentation, or simply in a discussion with friends. But in any situation, presenting a case with a sound logical argument carries more weight than simply stating a opinion.

Logic
IN PRACTICE

WINNING ARGUMENT

Lawyers acting on behalf of their clients base their cases on the evidence available, and how it relates to the law of the land. To convince a judge or jury, however, and prove their case beyond a reasonable doubt, they must present a logical argument, and point out the inconsistencies of opposing arguments.

MONEY MATTERS

The economic policies of opposing political parties are often very different, yet all claim to offer the best way to achieve prosperity. To decide between them, we must assess both the strength of their arguments, and the logical implications of their policies.

In any task, it is useful to organize your thoughts in a clear and logical way, but it is especially helpful in studying and learning. Tackling a project or preparing for an exam is more effective when done methodically, and the information is easier to understand and remember if it follows a logical course.

LOGICAL LEARNING

SCIENTIFIC PROGRESS

The natural sciences are based on a process of inductive reasoning, deriving theories from observation and experiment. The methods used to test these theories are constantly being refined, exposing the weaknesses in existing theories, but also paving the way for new discoveries that drive scientific progress.

Logic developed as a means of presenting and analyzing philosophical arguments, but the principles of logic can be applied to arguments supporting any belief or theory. We can apply rational thought—our ability to reason—to almost everything, and logic provides a framework for how we think.

Claims are often made about alternative medicine, special diets, or "superfoods," promising miraculous results. If they seem too good to be true, it's because there is little evidence that they actually work. Before they can be considered effective—and safe—treatments need to be tested using proper scientific methods.

BAD SCIENCE

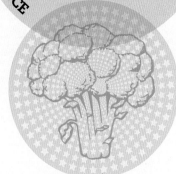

MIGHTY MACHINES

Logic is vital for computer science and information technology. Programming a machine to do a task requires breaking it down into a logical series of steps, and advances in mathematical logic have led to an ever wider range of applications for computer technology, as well as increased security (such as protection from identity theft).

What is **RIGHT** and **WRONG**?

There's no such thing as GOOD and BAD

What is a GOOD LIFE?

RIGHT and WRONG: It's all relative...

Do the ends JUSTIFY the means?

What kind of SOCIETY do you want to live in?

What makes a society CIVILIZED?

Is it possible to have FREEDOM and JUSTICE?

We don't have EQUAL rights

What's GOD got to do with it?

Are we playing GOD?

What is ART?

Moral philosophy, or ethics, is the area of philosophy concerned with what actions are right or wrong in various circumstances, and the best way for us to lead our lives. Closely connected is the branch of political philosophy, which is concerned with ideas such as justice and liberty, and how we can organize and govern our societies.

HURRAH!

"THIS IS GOOD"
EXPRESSES APPROVAL...

There's no as GOOD

MUCH OF PHILOSOPHY IS CONCERNED WITH QUESTIONS ABOUT THE WORLD AROUND US AND OUR UNDERSTANDING OF IT, AND CAN SEEM TO HAVE LITTLE TO DO WITH OUR DAY-TO-DAY LIVES. THE BRANCH OF PHILOSOPHY KNOWN AS MORAL PHILOSOPHY, OR ETHICS, HOWEVER, EXAMINES OUR IDEAS OF RIGHT AND WRONG, GOOD AND BAD, AND THE MORAL BASIS FOR OUR JUDGMENTS AND ACTIONS.

What is virtue?

Like other areas of philosophy, moral philosophy emerged as an attempt to find a rational explanation for beliefs that were simply accepted by convention. Ideas of good and bad were generally dictated by religion or tradition, with laws describing right or wrong behavior. But philosophers such as Socrates weren't content to accept the rightness or wrongness of an action. They tried to identify the properties of these actions that make them morally either good or bad. Socrates approached the problem by challenging conventional ideas. By asking the fundamental question "What is virtue?" he sought to define the moral properties of good and bad that we use as a basis for judging whether our actions are morally right or wrong. Moral philosophy tries to identify these moral properties by rational argument, in order to provide reasonable grounds for our ethical judgments.

THE RULES OF MORALITY, THEREFORE, ARE NOT CONCLUSIONS OF OUR REASON.

DAVID HUME

See also: 14–15, 110–111

PERSONAL AND POLITICAL

The field of ethics, or moral philosophy, examines the ways we can judge whether an action is morally good or bad. In addition to deciding our own individual moral code—what we think is right or wrong—together we establish laws based on ethical judgments. These not only prevent crimes and injustices, but determine how we govern our societies—the political systems.

such thing and **BAD**

… AND "THIS IS BAD" EXPRESSES DISAPPROVAL.

BOO!

The is/ought problem

David Hume, however, was unconvinced that morality can be judged by reasoned argument. By reasoning, we can demonstrate how something is, but, Hume argued, this is different from saying how it ought to be—there is a difference between the world of fact and the world of value. We can't derive an "ought" from an "is," so reason cannot be a basis for moral judgments. He felt that much of moral philosophy made the mistake of establishing facts by reasoning, and then inferring a moral value with no justification: Rules of morality cannot be conclusions of a reasoned argument. Hume believed that what he called "passions"—our emotions and instinctive drives—shape our ideas and behavior, which we then justify by *reasoning*. Similarly, we have a "sentiment," a moral sense, which guides our ethical decisions, and it is from this that we derive our moral rules.

Boo! Hurrah!

Other philosophers were also skeptical about whether reason could underpin moral rules. Echoing Hume's ideas, British philosopher A. J. Ayer suggested in the 1930s that statements about morality might seem to state facts, but in reality they just express attitudes. A moral rule, such

Thumbs down ❷
David Hume and A. J. Ayer believed that we cannot reason about morality because our own subjective feelings will determine whether or not we consider an action or opinion to be morally right or wrong.

the word *morality* comes from the Latin word *moralitas*, which means "proper behavior."

as "Killing is wrong," looks as though it states a true fact. According to Ayer, however, all it does is express an attitude of disapproval toward killing—like saying "Boo to killing!" It doesn't actually state anything. The same is true of "Charity is good." This expresses how the speaker feels about charity ("Hurrah to charity!"), but, like "Killing is wrong," it has no real meaning, and is neither true nor false. Ayer argued that all so-called moral rules are meaningless—they can only ever express a person's emotions. On the other hand, "I disapprove of killing" is a meaningful claim. It states a fact about oneself, and this fact could be false (it could be a lie). Ayer's theory is known as expressivism, or the "Boo/Hurrah theory." Like Hume, Ayer thought that morality is rooted in our emotions.

What is a GOOD LIFE?

WE USE OUR MORAL JUDGMENT TO DECIDE WHAT WE CONSIDER GOOD AND BAD, AND HOW WE SHOULD ACT IN CERTAIN SITUATIONS. WE ALSO USE MORE GENERAL IDEAS ABOUT WHAT CONSTITUTES MORALLY CORRECT BEHAVIOR AS A GUIDE TO THE WAY WE LEAD OUR LIVES. AND PERHAPS LEADING A MORALLY GOOD LIFE MEANS THAT IT CAN BE A HAPPY ONE, TOO.

> IT IS IMPOSSIBLE TO LIVE WISELY AND HONORABLY AND JUSTLY WITHOUT LIVING PLEASANTLY.
>
> EPICURUS

See also: 118–119, 124–125, 128–129

Leading a life of virtue

An important part of ancient Greek culture was the idea of the "good life" that each person should aim to lead. The Greeks had a word for it: *eudaimonia* (literally meaning "good spirit"), which embodied the idea of not only a morally correct way of life, but also a contented or happy one—what we today would consider a fulfilled life. Acting in a morally correct way leads to that kind of fulfillment because we feel satisfied in acting according to our principles, and feel uneasy when doing something we regard as ethically wrong. Philosophers sought to determine what it is that makes things morally good or bad, and to define *virtue*, which was central to living a good and happy life.

Achieving our full potential

Ancient Greeks used the word *arete*, which we translate as "virtue," but which, in fact, has a broader meaning, connected with the notion of the "good life." In addition to conveying the idea of moral correctness, *arete* conveys the notion of excellence, and the idea that it is "virtuous" to aim to achieve one's full potential. Socrates argued that in order to act virtuously, it is

THE NATURALISTIC FALLACY

According to G. E. Moore, ethical notions such as "good" and factual notions such as "pleasurable" should not be confused. It is a mistake to think that "good" means the same thing as "pleasurable," which describes a natural property of something. Ethical terms are not factual—they do not refer to things in the natural world, but describe non-natural properties, which we recognize by intuition, or moral sense.

VIRTUE

SENSUAL PLEASURES

A GOOD LIFE

 Diogenes the cynic rejected earthly pleasures so completely that he slept in a barrel.

necessary to know what *arete* is—the properties that make up virtue. To have that knowledge is to be virtuous; you cannot know *arete* and not lead a virtuous life. And people who behave incorrectly only do so because they do not know what virtue is. *Arete*, he concluded, is necessary and sufficient for the "good life": If you do not know what virtue is, you cannot lead a correct and fulfilling life, but if you do, you cannot lead anything other than a correct and fulfilling life.

Virtue or pleasure?

Other philosophers, notably Aristotle, agreed that virtue is necessary for a good and happy life, but said that it is not sufficient on its own. There are other good things that contribute to leading a fulfilled life, such as friends and family, health, and material comfort. There are also things that give us pleasure, such as wealth and power. Epicurus went so far as to argue that pleasure is the greatest good, and pain the greatest bad. He thought that morality can be measured by the amount of pleasure or pain it

causes, and so the aim of a good life is to maximize pleasure and minimize pain. But this was a minority view, and other schools of thought adopted Socrates's view. The Cynics, for example, advocated living a simple life of virtue in accordance with nature, rejecting all purely sensual pleasures. Later on, the Stoics developed this idea further, advocating a purely virtuous life in which external factors giving us pleasure, such as health, wealth, and power, are irrelevant, and those bringing us pain are to be tolerated. The division between these strands of thought resurfaced among later moral and political philosophers, who disagreed as to whether the morality of an action should be judged by its consequences, or its intentions.

FULFILLED

VIRTUOUS

HAPPY

◉ A good life is a happy life
Although Socrates, the Cynics, and the Stoics equated a good life with a virtuous one, Aristotle and Epicurus felt that we need both virtue and sensual pleasures in order to feel fulfilled.

SOCRATES

469–399 BCE

Born in 469 BCE, the son of a stonemason and a midwife from the Greek city-state of Athens, Socrates is the first great figure of Western philosophy, yet he remains an enigma. He left no direct writings behind, so what we believe we know about him comes from the works of others, notably his former students Plato and Xenophon the historian.

All accounts of Socrates describe him as ugly: short and stocky, with bulging eyes that appeared as if he was always staring.

CAREER CHANGE

After working as a stonecutter, Socrates served in the Athenian army against Sparta during the Peloponnesian War. He fought in three campaigns, including the siege of Potidaea, where he saved the life of Alcibiades, an Athenian general. Returning home, he became a full-time philosopher, wandering in public and using the whole of Athens as his classroom.

THE SOCRATIC METHOD

Socrates talked to anyone willing to engage him, and his method for teaching and exploring topics became famous as the Socratic Method. He adopted a position of complete ignorance before asking searching and clarifying questions that exposed gaps in knowledge or the lack of logic in an argument. This helped a student achieve understanding.

THE PEOPLE WATCHER

Socrates focused his philosophy squarely on humankind. He maintained that ultimate wisdom comes from people knowing themselves. He saw himself as "a citizen of the world," not just of Athens. He believed that the best form of government was not democracy or dictatorship but government by those with the greatest ability—a view that angered some Athenians.

" The **life** which is **unexamined** is not worth **living**."

ON TRIAL

Socrates's outspoken views gained him political enemies in Athens, and in 400 BCE he was accused of corrupting the minds of his young students. He was found guilty at his trial in front of about 500 Athenian citizens and sentenced to death. He declined the chance to flee and became his own executioner a year later, drinking a cup of poisonous hemlock.

RIGHT and WRONG:

MOST PEOPLE WOULD AGREE WITHOUT HESITATION THAT CERTAIN THINGS, SUCH AS GENOCIDE AND TORTURE, ARE MORALLY WRONG, NO MATTER WHO YOU ARE. BUT IS THIS TRUE? SOME PHILOSOPHERS HAVE ARGUED THAT ALL MORALITY IS RELATIVE, DEPENDENT ON CULTURE, WHILE OTHERS MAINTAIN THAT THERE ARE AT LEAST SOME MORAL ABSOLUTES.

See also: 118–119, 120–121

Our values are subjective

While Socrates and other ancient Greek moral philosophers tried to identify the properties of virtue to establish what it is that defines morality, another group of thinkers emerged who believed that there was no single simple answer to the question of whether something is right or wrong. The Sophists were originally lawyers, who, for a fee, used their skills in rhetoric and debate to argue cases in the courts. Often, two opposing clients both claimed to be in the right. From this, Sophist philosophers such as Protagoras developed the notion that there is more than one side to every argument, and that ideas of right and wrong depend on our perception—morality is based on subjective values. What is deemed right or wrong is largely determined by the culture and traditions of a social group, so the morality of any assertion or action must be judged relative to what is considered acceptable by that group.

children have to be taught the difference between right and wrong—they learn the moral values of their own society.

It's up to you

The view that the rightness or wrongness of anything depends on the norms of different social groups is known as relativism. Different cultures have different customs, and attitudes about what is considered ethically correct can change over time. Slavery, for example, was morally acceptable in ancient Greece, but seems obviously wrong to us today. Likewise, opinion is

FREEDOM TO CHOOSE

Taking the opposite view from relativism, Immanuel Kant proposed that morality is based on reason, as science is, and moral laws, like scientific laws, can have no exceptions—something that reason shows is morally right must always be right. We should be guided by what he called the categorical imperative: "Act only according to maxims that you can will also to be universal laws."

THERE IS MORE THAN ONE SIDE TO AN ARGUMENT.

YES

It's all relative...

divided not only from country to country, but also within countries, about the moral justification for the death penalty. For the relativist, morality is simply what the individual or perhaps the majority of people in a certain time and place approve of. Looked at in this way, moral judgments are simply a matter of opinion or taste. When we feel something is morally wrong, that is true for us. For those who feel differently, it is false. There is no objective truth.

No, it's not all relative

Relativism has been used to justify greater tolerance of other people's views and customs, especially in a multicultural society. But it is difficult to accept the idea that we can't criticize any moral claims— for example, when deciding if it is right to condemn things such as brutal penal systems when these are acceptable in other cultures. If morality is simply a matter of cultural opinion, we have no grounds for criticizing even tyranny and genocide. Taken to its extreme, relativism would have us believe that "anything

MAN IS THE MEASURE OF ALL THINGS.

PROTAGORAS

goes," but although societies and individuals may disagree on many moral issues, certain things are almost universally considered wrong. Most people believe that there are such things as moral absolutes—for example, that stealing is wrong—and these are reflected in the ethics of each culture.

◉ A matter of opinion
Moral relativists argue that opinions of what is right or wrong differ from culture to culture, so there is no objective truth. But most people would disagree with this argument.

MAYBE

DON'T KNOW

NO

Do the ends JUSTIFY

FACED WITH AN ETHICAL PROBLEM, THERE ARE A NUMBER OF FACTORS WE MUST CONSIDER. WE MAY DECIDE TO ACT ACCORDING TO A STRICT MORAL CODE OF WHAT WE REGARD AS RIGHT OR WRONG, REGARDLESS OF THE CONSEQUENCES. ANOTHER OPTION IS TO EXAMINE THE CONSEQUENCES OF OUR DECISION: BUT ARE CONSEQUENCES ALL THAT MATTER, MORALLY SPEAKING?

> IT MUST BE UNDERSTOOD THAT A **PRINCE** CANNOT OBSERVE ALL THOSE THINGS WHICH ARE CONSIDERED **GOOD** IN MEN.
>
> NiCCOLÒ MACHiAVELLi

The outcome is everything

Ideas of morality were shaped by religion rather than philosophy during the medieval period. The holy scriptures of Judaism, Christianity, and Islam, believed to be the word of God, contained laws that specified what things were considered right and wrong. In Europe, the power of the Church began to wane during the Renaissance, and nations emerged that were ruled by secular leaders using human-made, rather than God-given, laws. Rulers generally had advisers, and one of these, the Italian Niccolò Machiavelli, wrote a notorious handbook for rulers,

The Prince, in which he suggested that conventional personal morality should not influence political decisions. A ruler must be prepared to act immorally (for example, by using violence or deceit) for the good of the state. Although he may well have been satirically describing what rulers do, rather than what they ought to do, Machiavelli's message that the ends justify the means was a very influential one. Morality, he implied, should be judged on the consequences of actions, rather than on the actions themselves.

> someone who has no moral principles can be described as "machiavellian."

Pleasing most people

From Machiavelli's time onward, the Church had less and less influence in the way society was organized, and moral philosophy was no longer simply used to justify religious rules of morality. Instead, philosophers suggested alternative models, based on reason rather than dogma, and ethical systems based on outcomes rather than moral absolutes appeared. Perhaps the most important of these was developed by the English philosopher Jeremy Bentham, who proposed that the morality of an action can be judged by weighing up its beneficial and harmful consequences. These, he suggested, can be measured by the amount of pleasure or pain they give, and by the number of people that are

THE GOLDEN RULE

At the heart of almost every system of moral philosophy, and most religions, is some version of the Golden Rule: "Do unto others as you would have them do unto you." This embodies the principle of reciprocity—that we should treat others as we would wish to be treated ourselves—and it applies to both intentions and outcomes.

> THE **GREATEST HAPPINESS** OF THE GREATEST NUMBER IS THE FOUNDATION OF MORALS AND LEGISLATION.
>
> JEREMY BENTHAM

the means?

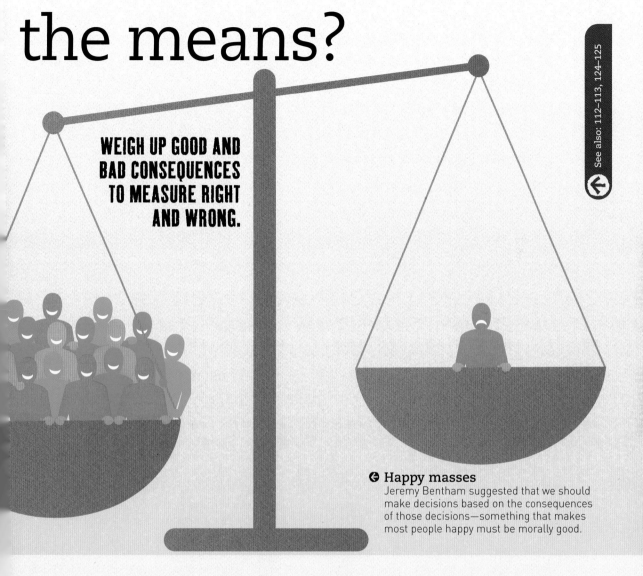

WEIGH UP GOOD AND BAD CONSEQUENCES TO MEASURE RIGHT AND WRONG.

See also: 112–113, 124–125

← **Happy masses**
Jeremy Bentham suggested that we should make decisions based on the consequences of those decisions—something that makes most people happy must be morally good.

affected—and the results could be calculated almost mathematically in what he called a "calculus of felicity." Something can be considered morally good if it maximizes pleasure and minimizes pain: What brings happiness to the greatest number of people is the measure of right and wrong.

We have a moral duty

Some philosophers, however, did not accept the idea of morality based on outcomes. Foremost among them was Immanuel Kant, who believed that something is either right or wrong, and there can

be no exceptions: Morality is a matter of duty, and should not be judged on consequences, no matter how harmful or beneficial they may be. If, for example, you believe that it is wrong to tell lies, Kant would argue that it is your moral duty to tell the truth at all times. Even telling a "white lie" to protect someone—for example, lying to a violent gang about where your friend is—is morally wrong. Kant stressed that we each have the freedom to decide what we consider to be morally correct, and must choose only those things that we are prepared to accept as unbreakable rules.

What kind of SOCIETY do you want to live in?

MORAL PHILOSOPHY IS CONCERNED WITH NOTIONS OF WHAT IS RIGHT AND WRONG, OR GOOD AND BAD, AND WHAT CRITERIA WE USE TO JUDGE MORAL ASSERTIONS. CLOSELY CONNECTED TO THESE IDEAS IS HOW THEY ARE APPLIED TO OUR SOCIAL BEHAVIOR, AND IN PARTICULAR HOW WE ORGANIZE OUR SOCIETIES— THE BUSINESS OF POLITICAL PHILOSOPHY.

the top 25 richest countries in the world are all representative democracies.

MAN IS BY NATURE A POLITICAL ANIMAL.
ARISTOTLE

The morals of city life

Western philosophy emerged in Greece at the same time that Greek civilization became established as a major cultural and political power. People settled in societies centered on a city-state, or *polis*, and various types of government evolved to organize them. In one *polis* in particular, Athens, philosophers turned their attention to questions of virtue and ethics, and then to the morality of the *polis* itself—its politics. The concept of what it means to lead a "good life" was seen to relate not only to individual citizens, but to the city-state as a whole. Civil societies like the *polis* need to be organized so that their citizens can lead "good" lives, but also to ensure that they can enjoy both justice and freedom. Political philosophy developed to examine not only the organization of societies, and the laws that determine their structure, but also how they are governed—who makes the laws, and how they are enforced.

❷ Playing for power

Aristotle defined forms of government according to who has power, and for whom that power is used. The white chess pieces represent what he saw as the virtuous forms, and the black pieces, the corrupt forms.

Philosophers rule

One of the first political philosophers was Plato, who gave a detailed description of what he considered an ideal society in his book *The Republic*. He wrote that people come together to form societies such as the *polis* in order to live a "good life," according to the notion of virtue. It is the purpose of the state, he suggested, to provide the means for them to do so. Ordinary citizens cannot simply be left alone to live virtuously because they have no knowledge of the ideal form of virtue, which can only be accessed through philosophical reasoning. For that reason, Plato asserted that the state should be ruled by an elite with the necessary knowledge—a class of philosopher-kings, who can guide and educate their subjects. The idea that ordinary people lack the necessary knowledge and skill to govern themselves persists today, even in

ARISTOCRACY

WHO'S IN CHARGE?

DEMOCRACY

representative democracies, in which a professional class of politicians has been elected to represent the views of the people.

Rules for you, or for the common good?

As in almost every aspect of philosophy, Aristotle took a very different stance from Plato in political matters. In his typically methodical way, Aristotle analyzed and classified the various possible forms of government, according to two criteria: Who rules, and on whose behalf? A state may be ruled by a single ruler, by a select group, or by the people as a whole. Those that ruled for the common good he called the "true" constitutions: monarchy, aristocracy, and polity (see right). By contrast, those that ruled in their own interest—tyranny, oligarchy, and democracy—

he described as "perverted" or "corrupt." On balance, Aristotle believed that polity (government by the citizens for the common good) is the ideal form of government, but democracy (government by the people in their own interest) is the least harmful of the corrupt forms. Today, most Western democracies would seem to confirm this assessment. But there are still many "corrupt" forms of government worldwide, and some theocracies (governed by religious officials in the name of God) have rejected the ideal of representative democracy.

See also: 120–121, 132–133

DEMOCRACY

Aristotle's view of democracy as "perverted" may seem puzzling, but he was referring to classical Athens, where only a certain class of men had the right to participate in the political process. Modern ideas of representative democracy— described by Abraham Lincoln as "government of the people, by the people, for the people"— are closer to Aristotle's "polity."

WHO'S IN CHARGE?

HANNAH ARENDT

1906–1975

Growing up in Königsberg (now Kaliningrad, Russia), Johanna "Hannah" Arendt lived close to the Russian-German border, which saw conflict during World War I. At the age of seven, she suffered a family tragedy when her father died. Arendt's passion for philosophy developed in her teens and she studied the subject in the 1920s at Marburg and Heidelberg Universities under noted thinkers Martin Heidegger and Karl Jaspers.

RISE OF THE NAZIS

Arendt witnessed the rise of the National Socialist (Nazi) Party in the early 1930s. As a Jew, she was barred from teaching at universities, and while researching Nazi propaganda techniques, she was arrested and interrogated by the Gestapo. Fearing imprisonment, Arendt fled to Paris in 1933, where she worked with refugee groups to help others leave Germany.

FLEEING OPPRESSION

When the Germans invaded France, Arendt was sent to a concentration camp, but she escaped and sailed with her husband, Heinrich Blücher, to the United States. There, she wrote her first major work, *The Origins of Totalitarianism* (1951), a landmark study of the dictatorial Nazi and Stalinist regimes, which she had experienced firsthand.

> "No **punishment** has ever possessed enough power of deterrence to **prevent** the commission of **crimes**."

THE HUMAN CONDITION

Arendt became a US citizen in 1951 and published *The Human Condition* seven years later. Looking back at philosophers from ancient Greece, the book discussed the classical ideals of work and citizenship. Arendt also defended personal political participation and freedom, and attacked the tendency of economics to dominate politics in modern societies.

A film called *Hannah Arendt* was released in 2013. It dramatizes Arendt's observations during the trial of Adolf Eichmann.

THE BANALITY OF EVIL

In 1961, Arendt observed part of the trial of Nazi war criminal Adolf Eichmann, one of the organizers of the genocide of six million Jews during World War II. In her 1963 book *Eichmann in Jerusalem*, Arendt caused controversy by arguing that Eichmann appeared "terrifyingly normal" and that atrocities were often not committed by evil monsters but by relatively ordinary people following orders unthinkingly.

What makes a society **CIVILIZED**?

Thomas Hobbes had good reason to want a strong leader—he lived through 20 years of civil war.

CIVILIZATIONS EVOLVED AS PEOPLE GATHERED TO LIVE IN INCREASINGLY BIG SOCIAL GROUPS, FIRST IN VILLAGES, AND THEN IN TOWNS, CITIES, AND NATIONS. THESE SOCIETIES OFFER ADVANTAGES, INCLUDING PROTECTION AND THE MEANS TO DEVELOP INDUSTRIES. ON THE OTHER HAND, WE MAY HAVE TO SACRIFICE SOME OF OUR FREEDOMS TO ENJOY A CIVILIZED LIFE.

A state of nature

Aristotle famously described man as a "political animal," meaning that he saw it as natural that we should want to live in societies such as the *polis*, the Greek city-state. Later philosophers, however, wanted to find out how these societies came about, in order to better understand how they should be organized. Thomas Hobbes took the approach of comparing life in a civilized society to life in what he described as a "state of nature." He took a dim view of nature, and especially human nature, and said that, left to their own devices, people would act simply in their own interest, and it would be a case of "every man for himself." In the world Hobbes envisioned, everyone would be pitted against

See also: 128–129

> ## THE CONDITION OF **MAN** IS A CONDITION OF **WAR** OF EVERYONE AGAINST EVERYONE.
>
> **THOMAS HOBBES**

one another in a perpetual state of war, and no one would be able to create prosperity, let alone pursue the finer things in life. To avoid this scenario, people come together, giving up some of their freedom to do what they want in return for the protection of a civilized society.

The social contract

Civil societies are formed when such a reciprocal arrangement, or "social contract," exists between the citizens and some form of sovereign authority—a leader or government—which makes and enforces laws to protect the people and allow them to get on with their lives. Hobbes believed that to prevent the society from falling back into an anarchic (lawless) "state of nature," there has to be a strong leader, a monarch or sovereign protector, who is given authority by the people. John Locke, a generation later, accepted the notion of a social contract, but had a very different idea of the "state of nature." He believed that it was not a state of anarchy, and that people would naturally treat each other with respect,

REVOLUTION

The ideas of philosophers such as John Locke and Jean-Jacques Rousseau had a great impact on 18th-century politics, especially on the revolutions in France and America. Rousseau's views on restricted freedom were echoed in the *Communist Manifesto* by Karl Marx and Friedrich Engels, who called for workers to unite in socialist revolution: "you have nothing to lose but your chains."

even outside civil society. Indeed, they would behave according to a moral "law of nature," recognizing the natural rights of others to food, water, shelter, and so on. Civil societies are formed not to restrict our rights, but to ensure them, and the social contract is the means by which the people can appoint a government to act on their behalf as an impartial judge in any conflicts. Rather than a strong leader, Locke concluded, the authority should be given by the people to an elected, representative government.

Power to the people

Jean-Jacques Rousseau proposed yet another view of the "state of nature," almost totally opposite from that of Hobbes. Rousseau believed that humans are born free, and can live in harmony with one another if left to make their own decisions. Civil societies, he argued, are not formed to protect rights and freedoms, but are constituted to protect property, and actually restrict our natural freedoms. Instead of the representative government advocated by Locke, he suggested giving power directly to the citizens. In Rousseau's system, laws would come from the people as a whole— what he called the "general will"— and would apply equally to all and work for the benefit of all.

❷ Society's chains

While Thomas Hobbes and John Locke cast society in a protective role, Jean-Jacques Rousseau argued that property ownership and other aspects of society have restricted our ability to control our own lives.

MAN WAS BORN FREE, YET EVERYWHERE HE IS IN CHAINS.
JEAN-JACQUES ROUSSEAU

CIVIL SOCIETY RESTRICTS OUR NATURAL FREEDOM.

People can't just go around killing

The question "What is justice?" is one that has occupied philosophers since the time of Socrates, and there have been many different interpretations of how society can be organized to ensure justice. Government of any kind imposes rules on a society—laws to protect the security of its citizens. For instance, every society has laws to prevent such things as murder and theft, and most would accept that it is just to deny people the right to go around killing and stealing, since it protects all of us from murderers and thieves. But the balance between how much a law protects individual rights and freedoms, and how much it restricts them, is seldom so clear-cut. Thomas Hobbes, for example, advocated an authoritarian government to protect life and property, while at the other extreme Jean-Jacques Rousseau felt that laws should be determined by the people for the benefit of society as a whole—an expression of freedom rather than a limitation.

> The principle of free speech allows us to say what we want as long as it doesn't harm others.

> ## THE ONLY FREEDOM WHICH DESERVES THE NAME IS THAT OF PURSUING OUR OWN GOOD IN OUR OWN WAY.
>
> JOHN STUART MILL

We should be free, within reason

Somewhere between these two extremes, John Stuart Mill established the principles of British liberalism. He was influenced by Jeremy Bentham's idea of utilitarianism, which asserted that morality should be judged by the greatest happiness of the greatest number. But Mill saw that applying this to politics presented practical problems: The happiness of the majority might impinge upon the happiness of some individuals. It was the job of society, he argued, to teach people to equate

Is it possible to have FREEDOM and JUSTICE?

FOR PEOPLE TO ENJOY THE BENEFITS OF A CIVIL SOCIETY, THERE HAVE TO BE LAWS GOVERNING THEM. ALTHOUGH THIS MEANS CITIZENS ARE NOT FREE TO DO WHATEVER THEY WANT, THESE LAWS PROTECT THEIR PROPERTY, THEIR SECURITY AND HEALTH, AND THEIR BASIC RIGHTS. TO BE ACCEPTED, HOWEVER, THE LAWS MUST BE CONSIDERED JUST.

their individual happiness with the common good, and act according to the principle "do as you would be done by." He believed that everyone should have the freedom to pursue their own happiness, but that society should impose one restriction, known as the "harm principle": people should be free to do what they want, as long as this does not harm others, or restrict their liberty. The only time a person's conduct concerns the state is when it affects society—and government, and the law, should only interfere with that person's freedom for the protection of society.

TAKE CONTROL OF YOUR DESTINY

Freedom, according to Isaiah Berlin, is not just freedom from external interference, from the "chains" imposed on us. This freedom *from* something is what he calls "negative freedom," but there is also a "positive freedom" that comes from within. This is the freedom we feel when we overcome things inside us that may hold us back, and are free to make our own choices in life.

Fairness or entitlement?

The definition of *justice* is still a topic of debate. American philosophers John Rawls and Robert Nozick have offered two different interpretations. For Rawls, justice is a matter of fairness—a fair distribution of rights, resources, and position in society. He asks us to imagine an ideal society, and how everything is distributed in it, but without knowing what position we would have in that society. This "veil of ignorance" (not knowing our position) stops us from being influenced by our own interest, so we create a fair society for all. For Nozick, on the other hand, justice is a matter of entitlement: There is justice when people are entitled to what they possess. Property must be justly transferred, and the government should only get involved to deal with cases when it is acquired by people not entitled to it, without the owner's consent—for instance, when something has been stolen.

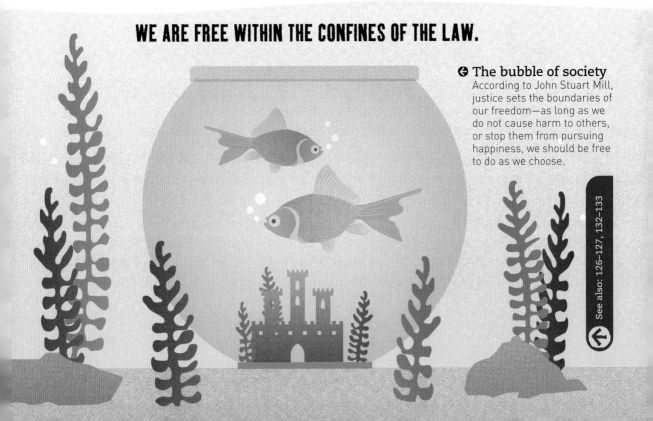

WE ARE FREE WITHIN THE CONFINES OF THE LAW.

⊙ The bubble of society
According to John Stuart Mill, justice sets the boundaries of our freedom—as long as we do not cause harm to others, or stop them from pursuing happiness, we should be free to do as we choose.

See also: 126–127, 132–133

We don't have

ONE OF THE MARKS OF A CIVILIZED SOCIETY IS THE WAY IT RESPECTS ITS CITIZENS' RIGHTS. AT THE END OF THE 18TH CENTURY, A TIME OF REVOLUTION, PHILOSOPHERS DEFINED WHAT THEY REGARDED AS THE BASIC HUMAN RIGHTS THAT THE LAWS OF SOCIETY SHOULD PROTECT. BUT IT WAS NOT UNTIL MUCH LATER THAT IT WAS RECOGNIZED THAT THESE SHOULD APPLY TO EVERYONE EQUALLY.

LIBERTY

SECURITY

PROPERTY

WE ARE ALL EQUAL, BUT SOME ARE MORE EQUAL THAN OTHERS.

The rights of man

The revolutionary movements in America and France sought to overthrow what were seen as unjust and oppressive rulers. With these rulers gone, the citizens were able to organize their new societies from scratch, inspired by philosophers such as John Locke and Jean-Jacques Rousseau. Central to their vision of how society should be governed was the recognition of certain fundamental rights. Echoing Locke, the US Declaration of Independence famously states: "We hold these truths to be self-evident, that all men are created equal, that they are endowed by their Creator with certain unalienable Rights, that among these are Life, Liberty and the pursuit of Happiness." And in France, the principle that all men are equal by nature and before the law, and have the right to liberty, security, and property, was made clear in the *Declaration of the Rights of Man and of the Citizen*. These rights were considered the minimum requirement for a civilized society.

⊘ It's not fair

Although men gained equal rights to liberty, security, and property in the 18th century, for women and ethnic minorities they were unattainable. Even today, inequality prevails.

EQUAL rights

The rights of woman

These declarations established a framework of rights to be enshrined in the constitution of society, and in both texts equality was seen as the first natural right. But although they are seen as the foundation of human rights legislation, the principle of equality only went so far in practice. Men were considered to have equal rights, but women were effectively excluded. Olympe de Gouges replied to the French declaration with her *Declaration of the Rights of Woman and the Female Citizen*, the opening shot in the battle for women's rights. Meanwhile, Mary Wollstonecraft's *A Vindication of the Rights of Woman* inspired a movement demanding rights for women, especially the right to education and participation in the political process. This movement grew through the 19th century, and eventually spawned the feminist movement led by Simone de Beauvoir.

> **FOR THE BLACK MAN THERE IS ONLY ONE DESTINY. AND IT IS WHITE.**
> FRANTZ FANON

> English philosopher and writer Mary Wollstonecraft was the mother of Mary Shelley, who wrote *Frankenstein.*

colonies, especially in Africa, and philosophers such as W. E. B. Du Bois and Frantz Fanon emerged with a specifically Afro-Caribbean political philosophy, inspiring a civil rights movement that did much to improve equality in the United States and elsewhere. Declarations of universal human rights were issued, and widespread condemnation of repressive regimes such as apartheid in South Africa led to eventual change. But many states still deny at least some of their citizens equal rights under the law. Even in Western democracies, where human rights are recognized in principle, people are treated far from equally in reality.

See also: 132–133, 134–135

Civil rights

Women were not the only ones excluded. Even after the abolition of slavery, black people were not considered to be citizens in many countries. The legacy of old empires also prevented equality in the

> **A WOMAN HAS THE RIGHT TO BE GUILLOTINED; SHE SHOULD ALSO HAVE THE RIGHT TO DEBATE.**
> OLYMPE DE GOUGES

CIVIL DISOBEDIENCE

The fight for equality has often led to violence, but rights movements have also succeeded using peaceful means. Many of the most effective, such as Gandhi's campaign against British rule in India, have been based on 19th-century philosopher Henry Thoreau's idea of civil disobedience. Thoreau felt that it is not only our right, but also our duty, to resist laws that go against our conscience through peaceful protest and noncooperation.

SIMONE DE BEAUVOIR

1908–1986

Simone-Lucie-Ernestine-Marie-Bertrand de Beauvoir was born in Paris in 1908. A precocious young woman intent on becoming a writer from an early age, she gained entry to the prestigious École Normale Supérieure. There, she joined a circle of influential male French philosophers, but would later carve out her own path, becoming a major philosophical influence on feminism.

SIMONE AND JEAN-PAUL

While studying philosophy in Paris, de Beauvoir met Jean-Paul Sartre. He would finish first and she came in a close second in the tough *agrégation* exams, with de Beauvoir the youngest to pass at the time. Despite rejecting his offer of marriage in 1929, de Beauvoir formed a lifelong relationship with Sartre. They reviewed each other's work and edited *Les Temps Modernes*, a literary journal, together.

De Beauvoir began work on *The Second Sex* in 1946, only a year after French women had their first opportunity to vote in elections.

"ONE IS NOT BORN, BUT RATHER BECOMES, A WOMAN"

First published in 1949, *The Second Sex* was an explosive 800-page study of the oppression of women throughout history. In the book, de Beauvoir charted how men had written almost all of the accounts of human nature and had defined maleness as the standard, with women defined only by how they met or differed from this standard.

> "**Representation** of the world, like the world itself, is the **work of men**; they describe it from their own point of view, which they confuse with the absolute **truth**."

STEREOTYPING WOMEN

De Beauvoir argued that women's attempts to achieve separate but equal status weren't helped by negative stereotypes in society, such as comparing a praying mantis with a powerful woman. *The Second Sex* attracted criticism and was placed on a banned books list by the Roman Catholic Church, but the work was popular, selling 20,000 copies in the first week.

NOVELIST, ACTIVIST

After teaching in schools from 1930 to 1943, de Beauvoir wrote extensively. Her output included travel books, recounting her visits to China, Cuba, and the United States, and novels such as the prizewinning *The Mandarins* and *The Coming of Age*, which criticized society for its treatment of the elderly. She also campaigned on issues including the legalization of abortion and Algerian independence from France.

IS EARTHLY SOCIETY A REFLECTION...

What's GOD got

CIVIL SOCIETIES CREATE LAWS THAT REFLECT THE MORAL PHILOSOPHY OF THEIR CULTURE. THESE ARE MEANT TO ENSURE THE WELFARE OF SOCIETY AS A WHOLE, AND PROTECT THE RIGHTS OF INDIVIDUALS. MANY RELIGIONS, HOWEVER, BELIEVE THAT MORALITY IS DICTATED BY GOD-GIVEN LAWS, AND THAT OUR LAWS SHOULD TAKE THESE COMMANDMENTS INTO ACCOUNT.

Laws and commandments

Moral and political philosophy had its origins in ancient Greece, where it was seen as largely separate from religion, and the gods had little to do with determining the rules of morality or the laws governing society. But with the advent of Christianity, religion once again had a huge impact on the laws of society in Europe, and Islam later had a similar influence on society in the Middle East. These religions taught that morality is not judged by reason, but dictated by commandments, which are the inviolable laws of God. While Islam gave more explicit instructions on the structure of society, Christian philosophers faced the problem of squaring God's laws of morality with the laws devised by humans to ensure the benefits of civil society. This became especially important as the Church became a political power during medieval times, and monarchs and popes were thought to have a divine right to rule.

The city of God

Among the earliest Christian philosophers was Augustine of Hippo, who had studied Greek philosophy before converting to Christianity. He used Plato's idea that the world we live in, the world of appearances, is merely a reflection of an ideal world (the world of forms), and argued that earthly society is a reflection of the kingdom of God. Our states and cities are imperfect, and governed by imperfect human-made

> christianity is the world's largest religion, followed by Islam, and then Hinduism.

> **REASON IN MAN IS RATHER LIKE GOD IN THE WORLD.**
> THOMAS AQUINAS

... OF THE KINGDOM OF GOD?

to do with it?

laws, but are modeled on an ideal "city of God." God has given us the power of reason to access knowledge of the laws of the city of God, and the freedom to model our own laws on them. Thomas Aquinas later suggested that God's eternal laws include what he called Natural Law, based on the morals, virtues, and values inherent in humans. Natural Law formed the basis for the laws of earthly society, but is incomplete, being only a part of God's law.

"God is dead"

After the Middle Ages, the Church lost much of its political control. Rulers whose power was given by a divine right were toppled, and states independent of the Church were established. In the process, the authority of God-given laws was questioned, and systems of government based on practicalities and human morality took its place. Political philosophy once again became largely separate from religion, and by the 19th century many philosophers were openly opposed to religion. Karl Marx saw religion as the "opium of the people"—a means of control and oppression, which prevented political progress—and, at the close of the century,

> **RELIGION IS THE SIGH OF THE OPPRESSED CREATURE, THE HEART OF A HEARTLESS WORLD, AND THE SOUL OF SOULLESS CONDITIONS.**
>
> **KARL MARX**

Friedrich Nietzsche pointed out the irrelevance of Judeo-Christian moral philosophy to the modern world by declaring that "God is dead." But societies still exist today whose laws are derived from religious laws (theocracies), and even modern secular democracies are built on principles inherited from their religious past.

See also: 20–21, 112–113

A JUST WAR?

Christianity and Islam are peace-loving religions, and killing and fighting are forbidden by their scriptures. Yet both faiths recognize the need to defend their religion and the existence of such a thing as a just war. Christian and Islamic philosophers came to similar conclusions about the requirements for a war to be just: rightful intention, just cause, proper authority, and the use of war only as a last resort.

Are we playing **GOD**?

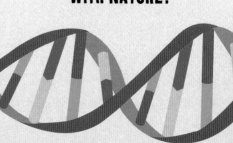

ADVANCES IN THE SCIENCES HAVE INCREASED OUR KNOWLEDGE OF THE
WORLD, BRINGING MANY BENEFITS. NOW, MORE THAN EVER BEFORE, WE
ARE ABLE TO CONTROL THE NATURAL WORLD TO OUR ADVANTAGE. MANY
OF THESE ADVANTAGES COME AT A COST, HOWEVER, AND WE SHOULD
CONSIDER THE MORAL IMPLICATIONS OF THIS SCIENTIFIC PROGRESS.

The morality of science

Questions of what is morally right and wrong are
closely connected to politics and the law, but moral
philosophy has a less obvious relevance to science. It
can be argued that scientific research and discoveries
are neither moral nor immoral, but that it is what uses
we make of them that determines whether they are
morally good or bad. Modern physics, for example,
explains such things as the relationship between
energy and matter, yet this knowledge has allowed
us to make nuclear power plants and nuclear
weapons. But even pure scientific research
involves some ethical decisions.
For example, some people wonder
whether or not it is morally defensible
to spend vast sums of money on
space exploration when so much
of the world's population lives in
extreme poverty. Sometimes, when
scientists and engineers find uses for
their discoveries that give
us more control over our
world—such as growing
genetically modified crops to
combat food shortages—these
are described as "unnatural,"
and our manipulation of natural
phenomena as "playing God."

Arab
physician Al-
Ruhawi wrote the
oldest surviving book on
medical ethics in the
9th century.

Life-and-death decisions

Although the idea of playing God is derived from the
morality dictated by many religions, even some
nonreligious people feel that there are some things
we should not meddle with. In medicine, for example,
we often need to make life-and-death decisions,
which pose ethical dilemmas. Euthanasia,
or "mercy killing," conflicts
with both religious

**IS IT MORALLY
RIGHT TO INTERFERE
WITH NATURE?**

THE **WORLD** DOES NOT BELONG TO **HUMANS.**

ARNE NAESS

COMMANDMENTS

The idea that God-given commandments determine human morality is deeply ingrained in Western culture, and is implied when we talk of life-and-death decisions as "playing God." But are laws commanded by God because they are morally good, or are they morally good because they are commanded by God?

commandments and the law, but in some cases, people may feel it is justified to put an end to a person's suffering. Opponents, using the "playing God" argument, say it is always wrong for a person to take another person's life—but this raises the question of whether or not it is morally right to leave someone to die in pain, rather than bring their life to a merciful end. This kind of ethical dilemma is becoming increasingly common as medical science provides us with ways of extending our lives—for example, machines that are capable of keeping us alive. Doctors and relatives often have to decide if a patient's life support should be switched off. And it could be argued that using a machine to keep someone alive who would otherwise be dead is also "playing God."

Shaping our environment

Other sciences also present us with ethical dilemmas. While medicine now enables us to extend life or end it painlessly, genetic engineering gives us

The first mammal ever to be cloned, Dolly the sheep, was born in Britain in 1996.

the power to modify and even create life. The benefits to humankind of providing a reliable source of food and developing ways of combating disease—for example, through animal testing—give some moral justification. Similarly, technology has created a safe and comfortable environment for us, but a growing number of scientists and philosophers are arguing that some of our actions are wrong, not because they break a moral law, but because of their unintended environmental consequences. Although our intentions—to make life better for people—may be good, these technological advances affect our environment and, in the long run, may be destructive. Norwegian environmentalist philosopher Arne Naess was among the first to suggest that we should live as an equal part of the natural world and should "think like a mountain"—considering not just the benefits and harm to people, or even other animals, but the long-term interests of the environment as a whole.

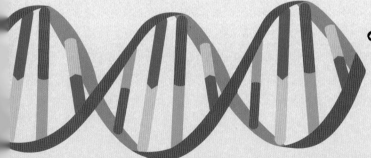

◷ Dabbling in DNA

Science has transformed the way we live: We can clone animals, and we can cure diseases. But at what point does all this become unethical? Some fear that dabbling with things as unpredictable as living organisms could potentially introduce disastrous and irreversible changes into the natural environment.

What is **ART?**

PHILOSOPHERS HAVE APPROACHED THE SUBJECT OF WHAT IS CONSIDERED BEAUTIFUL OR ARTISTIC—AESTHETICS—IN MUCH THE SAME WAY AS THEY HAVE APPROACHED MORALITY. SOME HAVE TRIED TO DEFINE THE PROPERTIES OF BEAUTY AND ART, WHILE OTHERS HAVE SUGGESTED THAT APPRECIATION OF THESE QUALITIES DEPENDS ON CULTURE, OR IS SIMPLY A MATTER OF TASTE.

> ## BEAUTY OF **STYLE** AND **HARMONY** AND **GRACE** AND GOOD RHYTHM DEPEND ON **SIMPLICITY**.
> **PLATO**

What makes something beautiful?

One of the seemingly simple questions that Socrates asked was "What is beauty?" He was not just seeking a definition of the word, but trying to see if there is some specific property that makes something beautiful—something inherent in all things that are beautiful. His pupil Plato argued that there is such a thing as ideal beauty, which exists in an ideal world of perfect forms (separate from the world we live in), and that we measure what we consider to be beautiful against that ideal. Aristotle, however, believed that we have developed our ideas of what constitutes beauty from our experience of all the different things we find beautiful. But people have very different ideas of what is beautiful, so perhaps beauty is not an inherent quality of things; rather, it is "in the eye of the beholder"—a matter of taste or opinion. Relativist philosophers suggest that ideas of beauty are shaped by culture and tradition. For example, most people consider the landscape of their homeland beautiful, regardless of what that landscape is.

☞ A work by vincent van gogh sold for $150 million in 1990. He only sold one painting in his lifetime.

Different times and places

We find beauty in things that are made by humans, such as works of art, as well as in the natural world. Plato had little time for the arts, and considered them to be a pale imitation of the ideal form of beauty. Aristotle, on the other hand, saw them as a reflection of nature and the instances of beauty in it, giving us insight as well as pleasure. Others believe that the arts are a product of culture and tradition, and that what is considered artistically beautiful or meaningful has been different at different times and in different places. For example, Classical Greece (the time of Plato and Aristotle) produced great works of poetry, theater, music, architecture, and art, which displayed certain common characteristics—notably proportion, symmetry, balance, and harmony. These reflected not just nature, but a cultural tradition that valued rational thought, math, logic, and social order. But other cultures reflect different interpretations of the natural world, producing very different styles of artistic expression, and different notions of what constitutes the value of a work of art.

WHAT'S IN A NAME?

If a painting by a famous artist, considered an example of his or her best work, turns out to be a fake, or the work of a lesser painter, its monetary value drops and it is no longer considered so great. The picture remains the same; only the "label" we attach to it has changed—yet this appears to override other criteria for considering it great.

An objective appraisal?

Modern artists have challenged our conventional ideas of what art is. Sometimes, the public is baffled by the work of avant-garde artists, and question if it should be called art at all. One traditional view is that art is something that is made by someone with the intention of conveying an idea or emotion—but looking for such intentions may color our opinion of it. Writer and philosopher Susan Sontag thought that a work of art should be appraised on its own merits, ignoring the artist's intentions. An alternative way to define art is by the value placed on it by so-called experts in the field (see What's in a name?, below left). In short, it is simply a matter of opinion or taste. And if that's the case, perhaps there is no objective way to appraise a work of art.

> ONE DOESN'T NEED TO KNOW THE ARTIST'S PRIVATE **INTENTIONS.** THE **WORK** TELLS ALL.
>
> **SUSAN SONTAG**

See also: 20–21, 124–125

HOW DO WE JUDGE ART?
IS BEAUTY IN THE EYE OF THE BEHOLDER?

⬆ Like what you see?

Philosophers have tried to establish whether a work of art is beautiful in its own right, or whether it is our individual experience of that work that makes it beautiful.

CRIME AND PUNISHMENT

What society considers right or wrong is reflected in its laws, and justice is applied when they are broken. Society must decide what sentence is appropriate and if its goal is to punish, to deter, or to protect the public. It must also assess the morality of sentences such as the death penalty.

THINK TANKS

The laws that govern democratic societies are made by politicians, elected to represent the people. But these representatives can't be experts in everything, and in order to make informed judgments, they rely on expert advice. Think tanks, groups of policy advisors, examine the ethics of a policy as well as the practicalities.

Moral and political philosophy
IN PRACTICE

ANIMAL TESTING

Scientists are constantly trying to find treatments for diseases such as cancer. Some researchers maintain that animal testing is needed to ensure that treatments are safe, and that it is justified by the benefits to humans. But animal rights activists argue that this testing is morally wrong, and that there are alternatives.

DISTRIBUTION OF WEALTH

A government's economic policy should ensure the prosperity of the state. Through its tax and welfare systems, the government also decides how the country's resources are shared—the contributions and entitlements of its citizens. Often, it has to seek a balance between creating wealth and ensuring its fair distribution.

The directors of a company often have difficult decisions to make. Their main concern is to ensure that the business is successful and makes money for the company and its shareholders. But they must also consider the customers, providing a good product or service at a fair price, and the rights of their workers to fair pay and working conditions.

BALANCING BUSINESS

HUMAN RIGHTS

In many countries, citizens' rights are written into the constitution, but a Universal Declaration of Human Rights was adopted by the United Nations in 1948. This has since been signed by most countries and is now effectively part of international law, but it is constantly being extended as further rights are recognized.

It is perhaps easier to see the relevance of moral and political philosophy to the everyday world than any other branches of philosophy. Decisions involving right and wrong have to be made in every walk of life, from the formal verdicts of courts of law to our personal lifestyle choices.

Most countries are represented in organizations such as the United Nations, where they discuss global relations, try to resolve conflicts, and decide on matters including war crimes. Peacekeeping forces may be organized, but there is often debate about whether it is right to interfere in a country's internal affairs.

KEEPING THE PEACE

THE WAR ON TERROR

Lately, governments around the world have responded to acts of terrorism by increasing security. At airports and in public places, there are more restrictions and increased surveillance. But with security cameras everywhere, and our Internet activity being monitored, many people are asking if this loss of privacy is proportionate to the threat.

Directory of philosophers

Anaximander (c. 610–c. 546 BCE)
Anaximander came from Miletus, a busy port in ancient Greece. His theories were influenced by the Greek mythical tradition and by Thales. Also interested in astronomy, geography, and biology, he was the first ancient Greek to draw a map of the known world, and came up with a theory that people had evolved from fish.

Anaximenes (c. 585–c. 528 BCE)
Like Thales and his teacher Anaximander, Anaximenes was from Miletus, in what is now Turkey. He is best known for his idea that everything is primarily made of air. As air got thicker, he said, it turned to wind, then cloud, then water, then mud and stones.

St. Anselm (1033–1109)
St. Anselm was born in Aosta, in the Italian Alps. When he was 27, he joined the Benedictine Abbey at Bec in Normandy, France. He became the abbot in 1078, and from 1093 to 1109 he held the office of archbishop of Canterbury in England. Anselm is famous for his ontological argument for the existence of God.

Hannah Arendt (1906–1975) See 130–131

Aristotle (384–322 BCE) See 96–97

Augustine of Hippo (354–430)
Augustine was brought up as a Christian in what is now Algeria, but his philosophy studies at Carthage left him dissatisfied with his religion. He later converted back to Christianity, and developed his philosophy (based on Plato's world of forms) that earthly society is an imperfect reflection of the kingdom of God. After time in Italy, he returned to North Africa and became the bishop of Hippo.

Avicenna (Ibn Sînâ) (c. 980–1037)
Avicenna was born near Bukhara, in modern-day Uzbekistan. An important Islamic philosopher in the Middle Ages, he questioned whether our minds (or souls) are separate from our bodies long before René Descartes. He also contributed much to science—especially to medicine.

A. J. Ayer (1910–1989)
British philosopher Alfred Jules Ayer's *Language, Truth, and Logic* (1936) introduced logical positivism—the idea that a claim is only meaningful if it can be shown, by experience, to be true or false. Moral rules, he said, are meaningless, and just express emotions.

Francis Bacon (1561–1626)
Francis Bacon was born in London and studied at Cambridge University and Gray's Inn. He is famous for his philosophy of science, and has been called the creator of empiricism. In 1618 he became lord chancellor of England, and in 1621 he became Viscount St. Albans, before being jailed briefly for accepting bribes.

Simone de Beauvoir (1908–1986) See 138–139

Jeremy Bentham (1748–1832)
One of the founders of modern utilitarianism, English philosopher Jeremy Bentham is best known for his theory that advocates the greatest happiness of the greatest number. A child prodigy, he was sent to study law at Oxford at the age of 12. He was a social reformer, who fought for the decriminalization of homosexuality, believed in the equality of the sexes, and argued in favor of animal rights.

Henri Bergson (1859–1941)
Born in France, Henri Bergson had an English mother and a Polish father, both of whom were of Jewish descent. He studied in Paris, and although he excelled at math and science as well as the arts, he opted for a career in philosophy. He is best known for his work on the concept of time as it is actually experienced—"duration," or lived time—and was awarded the Nobel Prize for Literature in 1927.

George Berkeley (1685–1753)
Empiricist and Anglican bishop George Berkeley studied at Trinity College in Dublin, Ireland. There, influenced by the writings of John Locke and René Descartes, he wrote all of his best-known philosophical works. Berkeley took empiricism to extremes, arguing that nothing material exists—the only things we can be sure exist are ideas and the minds that perceive them.

Isaiah Berlin (1909–1997)
Isaiah Berlin was born into a Jewish family in Riga, in the Russian Empire (present-day Latvia). He spent the first part of his life in Russia, but due to rising anti-Semitism, his family soon emigrated to Britain. Berlin is best known for his political philosophy, in which he argued that we are free to make our own choices, and that the best kind of liberty comes from within. He was knighted in 1957.

W. E. B. Du Bois (1868–1963)
William Edward Burghardt Du Bois was the first African American to earn a PhD from Harvard. In addition to being a professor of history, sociology, and economics at Atlanta University and a prolific author, he was a key figure in the Civil Rights movement, fighting for equality for black people in a world ruled by whites.

Albert Camus (1913–1960)
Born in French Algeria, Albert Camus studied at the University of Algiers, and was influenced by the works of Søren Kierkegaard and Friedrich Nietzsche. He then moved to France, where he worked as a political journalist and also wrote fiction, essays, and plays. His philosophy was distinctly gloomy—he believed that there was no purpose to our existence, and that we should just accept that life is futile. In 1957, he was awarded the Nobel Prize for Literature, and died in a car accident just three years later.

Democritus (c. 460–c. 371 BCE)
Ancient Greek philosopher Democritus was born in Thrace, and, with his teacher Leucippus, came up with the idea of atomism (that everything is made of tiny, unchanging particles) . Although he was a modest man who lived for his work, he acquired fame for his ability to predict changes in the weather. He was known as the "laughing philosopher" due to his tendency to laugh at human folly.

René Descartes (1596–1650) See 72–73

John Dewey (1859–1952)
John Dewey was a major figure in American pragmatism. A great scholar, he studied at the University of Vermont before teaching at various leading universities. He wrote extensively on a range of topics, and set up the University of Chicago Laboratory Schools, which put into practice his philosophy of learning by doing.

Empedocles (c. 490–c. 430 BCE)
Greek thinker Empedocles's philosophy was rooted in the belief that there are four elements of matter: earth, air, fire, and water. All things are created from these elements, including humans. A follower of Pythagoras's ideas, he supported the doctrine of reincarnation, and followed a vegetarian diet.

Epicurus (341–270 BCE)
Epicurus was an ancient Greek philosopher. He believed that because in death we experience neither pleasure nor pain, it is our duty to maximize our happiness before we die. His school, which was based in the garden of his house, had a small but devoted following, and was the first of the ancient Greek philosophical schools to admit women as a rule rather than an exception.

Frantz Fanon (1925–1961)
Born in Martinique, Frantz Fanon studied medicine and psychiatry in France. In philosophy, he was influential in the field of postcolonial studies, and wrote about violence, corruption, and social control. He died at the age of 36; his last book, *The Wretched of the Earth*, was published posthumously with a preface by Jean-Paul Sartre.

Ludwig Feuerbach (1804–1872)
Ludwig Feuerbach was a German philosopher and anthropologist. He abandoned theology to study under Georg Hegel at the University of Berlin, although he eventually rejected Hegel's views. Feuerbach was a materialist, and many of his writings offer a critical analysis of religion. He famously denied the existence of God except as an idealized object of human consciousness.

Paul Feyerabend (1924–1994)
Philosopher of science Paul Feyerabend was born in Vienna, Austria. After high school, he was drafted into the army, and was decorated with an Iron Cross during World War II. After the war, he briefly wrote for the theater, but after returning to Vienna to study, he was influenced by Karl Popper. Feyeraband is known for his view that there is no such thing as the "scientific method" because the methods used in science change all the time.

Gottlob Frege (1848–1925)
Born in Germany, Gottlob Frege was a mathematician who transformed the discipline of philosophical logic, which had previously changed little since the time of Aristotle. Although he also studied physics and chemistry, and made contributions to the philosophy of language, Frege spent his whole working life teaching math and logic at the University of Jena.

Siddhartha Gautama (the Buddha) (c. 563–c. 483 BCE)
Siddhartha Gautama was born into a royal family in present-day Nepal. When he ventured beyond the palace for the first time, he was shocked by the human suffering he saw, and sought ways to remedy it. Through meditation, he finally reached enlightenment—becoming the Buddha. Buddhism is based on his teachings.

Edmund Gettier (1927–)
Edmund Gettier is an American professor and epistemologist. He taught at Wayne State University in Michigan for 10 years, before moving to the University of Massachusetts, where he remains. Gettier is best known for a three-page paper he published in 1963, entitled "Is Justified Belief True Knowledge?"

Olympe de Gouges (1748–1793)
Olympe de Gouges was born Marie Gouzes in southern France, but reinvented herself when she moved to prerevolution Paris to seek fame as a writer. A self-educated woman, she wrote plays, novels, and pamphlets, and fought passionately for the rights of women and against slavery. Her outspokenness would eventually lead to her arrest, conviction, and execution by guillotine.

Georg Hegel (1770–1831)
Georg Hegel was born in Stuttgart, Germany, and studied theology at Tübingen. Turning to philosophy, he lectured at Jena University. His philosophy encompasses all of history, thought, and reality in one system. He was appointed to the chair of philosophy at Heidelberg and later Berlin, but died at the height of his fame.

Martin Heidegger (1889–1976)
An inspiring lecturer, German-born philosopher Martin Heidegger was appointed rector of Freiburg University in the 1930s. He also joined the Nazi Party, which led to him being banned from teaching after the war. In his best-known work, *Being and Time*, he wrote that we don't just experience time—our being *is* time.

Heraclitus (c. 536–c. 470 BCE)
Heraclitus was born in the ancient Greek city of Ephesus. He believed that the universe is constantly changing, and his ideas later influenced Plato's work. A grouchy man, he went to live in the mountains to escape the corruption of society. When he developed dropsy, he tried to cure himself by burying himself up to the neck in cow manure. It didn't work—he died from heat exhaustion instead.

Thomas Hobbes (1588–1679) See 80–81

David Hume (1711–1776) See 22–23

Edmund Husserl (1859–1938)

Born in Moravia in what is now the Czech Republic, Edmund Husserl studied astronomy and math before taking up philosophy. He eventually became a professor in Freiburg, Germany, but was suspended from teaching in 1933 under the Nazi regime because of his Jewish background. Husserl was the founder of phenomenology—the study of experience.

Hypatia (c. 355–415)

Born in Alexandria, Eygptian philosopher Hypatia was the leading astronomer and mathematician of her time. Her philosophy revolved around her belief in a divine being, "the One"—the ultimate source of all reality. Denounced by Christians and Jews as a pagan, Hypatia was brutally murdered by Christian zealots.

William James (1842–1910)

William James was born into a wealthy and influential New York family. His father was a philosopher, and his brother, Henry, became a renowned novelist. He earned a medical degree at Harvard (although he never practiced), and went on to teach medicine, psychology, and philosophy. A pragmatist, James argued that we should accept beliefs as long as they are useful; he also studied consciousness, describing it as a continually changing process.

Immanuel Kant (1724–1804) See 30–31

Søren Kierkegaard (1813–1855)

Søren Kierkegaard was born into a wealthy family in Denmark, and his large inheritance enabled him to dedicate his life to philosophy. His melancholic disposition is reflected in his philosophical beliefs—that we are free to shape our own lives, but this freedom will not necessarily bring us happiness. On this basis, he chose not to marry his fiancé, and died a recluse.

Kong Fuzi (Confucius) (551–479 BCE)

Kong Fuzi was an aristocratic Chinese thinker and educator, famous for his observations on society. At the age of 15, he decided to devote his life to learning, and went on to develop a social and political philosophy that is often considered to be the foundation of subsequent Chinese thought.

Thomas Kuhn (1922–1996)

American philosopher Thomas Kuhn earned a PhD in physics from Harvard, and then went on to study the philosophy of science. He is best known for arguing that scientific fields undergo periodic "paradigm shifts" (when a breakthrough results in a complete change of thinking), rather than solely progressing in a linear way.

Gottfried Leibniz (1646–1716)

German philosopher and mathematician Gottfried Wilhelm Leibniz is known for his work in metaphysics and logic. He had a career as a politician and diplomat, among other things, and studied philosophy, law, geology, physics, and engineering in his spare time. Independently of Isaac Newton, he also discovered calculus, but was not credited for this achievement in his lifetime.

John Locke (1632–1704)

John Locke was born in England, the son of a country lawyer. He studied medicine at Oxford University, where he also later taught. It was the work of René Descartes that inspired Locke to pursue philosophy. The first of the great British empiricist philosophers, he is known for his efforts to establish the limits of human knowledge, as well as for his work in political philosophy.

Niccolò Machiavelli (1469–1527)

Niccolò Machiavelli was an Italian politician and diplomat, who spent his life in Florence. He later devoted himself to political writing, and is regarded as a founder of modern political science. *Machiavellian* is a negative term widely used to characterize unscrupulous politicians of the type Machiavelli described in *The Prince*, his most famous work, which is presented as a handbook for princes on how best to rule in their own interest.

Karl Marx (1818–1883)

Karl Marx was a German economist and philosopher whose work had a radical impact on 20th-century history. In 1843, he met his lifelong collaborator, Friedrich Engels; in 1848, they published their *Communist Manifesto*. Marx believed that the conflict between rich and poor lay at the heart of society's problems, and that property should belong to communities, rather than individuals.

John Stuart Mill (1806–1873)

Born in London, John Stuart Mill worked for the East India Company for 30 years, writing in his spare time. Mill's father, philosopher and economist James Mill, worked his son hard: John was proficient in Greek and Latin by the age of seven, and later adopted the utilitarian outlook of his father and Jeremy Bentham. His wife, Harriet Taylor, reinforced his belief in equality for women, and helped him write *On Liberty*, which he dedicated to her.

G. E. Moore (1873–1958)

British philosopher George Edward Moore studied at Cambridge University, and later taught there alongside Bertrand Russell and Ludwig Wittgenstein—in the so-called "golden age" of Cambridge philosophy. He is known for advocating common-sense concepts, and for his contributions to ethics, epistemology, and metaphysics.

Arne Næss (1912–2009)

Born in Oslo, Norway, Arne Næss earned his doctorate in philosophy at the city's university. He later became an influential figure in the environmental movement, developing the notion of "deep ecology": the idea that all of nature matters and deserves equal consideration—not just the parts that impinge on humans.

Friedrich Nietzsche (1844–1900)

Friedrich Nietzsche was born in Germany, the son of a Lutheran pastor. He is famed for challenging Christianity, and argued that we are held back from realizing our true potential by religion and the fear of divine retribution. He became a professor at the age of just 25, but his life was dogged by physical and mental illness, and his philosophy was largely overlooked until the 20th century.

Robert Nozick (1938–2002)
Robert Nozick was born in Brooklyn, New York. He received a PhD in philosophy at Princeton University, and went on to teach there and at Harvard. He is best known for his book *Anarchy, State, and Utopia* (1974), a libertarian answer (promoting the rights of the individual) to his colleague John Rawls's *A Theory of Justice* (1971).

William of Ockham (c. 1287–1347)
William of Ockham is believed to have been born in Ockham, a village in southeast England. A Franciscan friar, he studied theology at Oxford University, and later taught there. His logical principle that, all things being equal, we should always choose the simplest explanation later became known as Occam's razor.

Parmenides (c. 515–c. 450 BCE)
Ancient Greek philosopher Parmenides was born in Elea, in what is now southern Italy. He was influenced by Xenophanes, and founded the Eleatic school of philosophy. His only known work is an epic metaphysical poem entitled *On Nature*, but he is also featured in a dialogue by Plato, who was greatly influenced by him.

Charles Sanders Peirce (1839–1914)
Charles Sanders Peirce was born in Cambridge, Massachusetts. His father was a brilliant mathematician and astronomer. Primarily a scientist, Peirce believed that philosophical debate should concentrate on finding satisfactory explanations, rather than truths, and founded the school of pragmatism on this basis. He had a lifelong friendship with fellow pragmatist William James.

Plato (c. 420–347 BCE) See 48–49

Karl Popper (1902–1994)
Born in Austria to Jewish parents, Karl Popper emigrated to New Zealand in 1937 when the Nazi Party threatened Austria's independence. He later became a British citizen. A renowned philosopher of science, he argued that progress is made in science through testing theories and eliminating those that prove to be untrue. He was knighted in 1965.

Protagoras (c. 490–c. 420 BCE)
Protagoras was born in Abdera, in ancient Greece, but spent most of his life in Athens. The greatest of the Sophists, a group of traveling teachers and intellectuals, he came up with the idea of relativism (that morality varies according to cultural or historical context). Legend has it that he was later accused of godlessness, and as a result his books were burned and he was exiled from Athens.

Hilary Putnam (1926–)
Hilary Putnam was born in Chicago, but spent his childhood in France before moving back to the United States. After studying math and philosophy, he earned a doctorate in philosophy. Putnam has had a distinguished academic career: He was made a fellow of the American Academy of Arts and Sciences in 1965, and elected president of the American Philosophical Association for 1976. His best-known work is on the philosophy of mind.

Pythagoras (c. 570–c. 495 BCE)
Pythagoras was the first person to use math to try to explain the universe, and his mathematical theorems are still taught today. Born on the Greek island of Samos, he later moved to southern Italy, where he founded a philosophical and religious school. His many followers were committed to the pursuit of knowledge, and they lived and worked according to a strict set of rules, which included not being allowed to eat beans.

John Rawls (1921–2002)
John Rawls was born in Baltimore. He studied at Princeton University, and served in the army during World War II before returning to pursue a doctorate in moral philosophy. He then studied at Oxford University, where he was influenced by Isaiah Berlin. His major work, *A Theory of Justice* (1971), in which he promoted the idea of "justice as fairness," was important in the revival of the study of moral and political philosophy.

Jean-Jacques Rousseau (1712–1778)
Jean-Jacques Rousseau was born to a Calvinist family in Geneva, Switzerland. At age 16, he ran away from home to France, where he earned his living as a tutor, musician, and writer. He later became part of a famous group of French intellectuals that included Denis Diderot and Voltaire. Rousseau thought that society restricts our natural freedoms, and that without society we would live together in harmony. His controversial views later influenced the French Revolution, as well as modern political and sociological thought.

Bertrand Russell (1872–1970)
Bertrand Russell was born into an influential and liberal British aristocratic family. His godfather was John Stuart Mill. At Cambridge University, he was taught by Alfred North Whitehead, with whom he collaborated on *Principia Mathematica*. Russell later taught Ludwig Wittgenstein at Cambridge. In addition to being a key contributor to philosophical logic, epistemology, and the philosophy of mathematics, Russell was a renowned social activist. He was awarded the Nobel Prize for Literature in 1950.

Gilbert Ryle (1900–1976)
English philosopher Gilbert Ryle was born into a prosperous family. He studied at Oxford University, where he taught until World War II, when he volunteered and worked in intelligence. Ryle is known for criticizing the human tendency to view the mind as a nonphysical element of the body—what he called a "ghost in the machine" in his 1949 book *The Concept of Mind*.

Jean-Paul Sartre (1905–1980)
Existentialist Jean-Paul Sartre was born in Paris and studied philosophy at the École Normale Supérieure, where he met his lifelong companion, Simone de Beauvoir. He taught until World War II, when he served in the army and was briefly imprisoned before joining the resistance movement. After the war, Sartre's work became more and more political, although he continued to write plays and novels as well as philosophical titles. He was offered, but rejected, the Nobel Prize for Literature in 1964.

Arthur Schopenhauer (1788–1860)

Arthur Schopenhauer was born into a wealthy German family. He taught philosophy at the University of Berlin at the same time as Georg Hegel, whom Schopenhauer despised. A pessimistic thinker, he is best known for his book *The World as Will and Representation*, and the idea that reality is made up of a world we can experience (the world of Representation), and one we can't (the world of Will).

John Searle (1932–)

American philosopher John Searle is best known for his "Chinese room" thought experiment, which challenges the notion of a truly intelligent artificial intelligence. He is also widely noted for his contributions to the philosophy of language and the philosophy of mind, and has received many awards and honorary degrees.

Peter Singer (1946–)

Peter Singer's Jewish parents emigrated to Australia in 1938 to avoid Nazi persecution in their native Austria, and Singer was raised in Melbourne. A moral and political philosopher, he is best known for his views on animal rights, and his belief in the capacity of animals to suffer just as humans do. He has also addressed issues such as abortion, euthanasia, and social equality.

Socrates (469–399 BCE) See 122–123

Susan Sontag (1933–2004)

Born Susan Rosenblatt in New York, Susan Sontag earned her master's degree in philosophy at Harvard. She taught philosophy before becoming a full-time writer. She is known for her essays on modern culture, and especially for those on art and aesthetics, which focus on the problem of how we should interpret images.

Benedictus Spinoza (1632–1677)

Born in Amsterdam to Jewish parents, Baruch (later Benedictus) Spinoza's criticism of organized religion led to his rejection by the Jewish community at the age of 23. A rationalist, he was influenced by René Descartes, and many of his ideas were so radical that they could only be fully published after his death. He lived a frugal life and died young of consumption, probably as a result of inhaling dust while earning his living as a lens grinder.

Harriet Taylor (1807–1858)

Harriet Taylor was born in London. She is known for her writing on women's rights, sexuality, and politics, and her belief that women should be allowed to live and work in the same "spheres" as men. She married John Stuart Mill after a long affair, and much of Taylor's writing was printed under Mill's name.

Thales of Miletus (c. 624–c. 546 BCE)

Very little is known about Thales, who is generally considered the first Western philosopher. He lived in Miletus, where he was born, but none of his writings survive. He is referred to in some detail by both Aristotle and Diogenes Laertius, however, and is recognized for his claim that everything is ultimately composed of water.

Henry Thoreau (1817–1862)

Henry David Thoreau was born in Concord, Massachusetts, and was educated at Harvard. He worked as a teacher, and then at his father's pencil factory, while intermittently living on the estate of his friend and mentor Ralph Waldo Emerson. He wrote more than 20 volumes on philosophy and natural history, which contributed to the later movement of environmentalism. The ideas in his essay "Civil Disobedience" influenced numerous leaders of resistance movements, including Mahatma Gandhi and Martin Luther King.

Alan Turing (1912–1954)

A pioneer of artificial intelligence, English mathematician and logician Alan Turing created what later became known as the Turing test to establish whether or not machines are capable of thought. During World War II, he played a central role in deciphering messages encrypted by the German Enigma machine. He was prosecuted for homosexuality (then a criminal offense) in 1952, and committed suicide two years later.

Alfred North Whitehead (1861–1947)

Born in Kent, England, Alfred North Whitehead studied math at Cambridge University and then spent 25 years teaching there. Among his students was Bertrand Russell, and the two became friends and later collaborated on the renowned work of mathematical logic *Principia Mathematica*. Whitehead gradually turned his attention from math to the philosophy of science, and finally to metaphysics.

Ludwig Wittgenstein (1889–1951) See 106–107

Mary Wollstonecraft (1759–1797)

Mary Wollstonecraft was born in London, the daughter of a farmer, and is regarded as one of the founding feminist philosophers. She is best known for *A Vindication of the Rights of Woman* (1792), in which she argues that women are not naturally inferior to men, but may appear to be so because they do not receive adequate education. She died at the age of 38, ten days after giving birth to her second daughter, Mary Shelley, the author of *Frankenstein*.

Xenophanes (c. 560–c. 478 BCE)

Xenophanes was born in Colophon, in ancient Greece, but lived a nomadic lifestyle. A poet and religious thinker, his philosophy was expressed in his poetry, and he gained a reputation for criticizing the immorality of the Greek gods and goddesses. He also made some pioneering reflections on the nature of knowledge. He is mentioned in the writings of both Plato and Aristotle.

Zeno of Elea (c. 495–c. 430 BCE)

Greek philosopher and mathematician Zeno of Elea is best known for his paradoxes, and especially for his efforts to demonstrate that movement is impossible. Aristotle called him the "father of the dialectic," doubtless a testament to his arguing skills. Zeno was a staunch supporter of his teacher Parmenides's claim that the universe is made of a single unchanging substance.

Glossary

Aesthetics
A branch of philosophy concerned with what is considered beautiful or artistic.

Analytic proposition
The opposite of a *synthetic proposition*—one that is true by virtue of the meaning of the words used to express it, such as "All stallions are male."

Anthropomorphism
Attributing human behavior or characteristics to something that is not human, such as an animal.

Arete
In ancient Greek philosophy, this comprises excellence and virtue.

Argument
In *logic*, a process of *reasoning* that infers a *conclusion* from one or more *premises*. The *premises* are supposed to support the *conclusion*.

Conclusion
The final part of a logical *argument* that is inferred from the *premises*.

Consequentialism
The view in *moral philosophy* that the *morality* of an action should be judged on its outcomes.

Contingent truth
Something that may or may not be the case—the opposite of a *necessary truth*.

Contradictory
Two statements are contradictory when the truth/falsity of one *entails* the falsity/truth of the other. If one is true, the other must be false.

Contrary
Two statements are contrary if they cannot both be true, but they may both be false.

Deduction
Drawing a particular *conclusion* from a general rule. An *argument* based on deduction is always valid, unlike its opposite, *induction*.

Dialectic
In ancient Greece, a method of pursuing truth by discussing ideas with people holding differing views.

Dualism
The view that there are two kinds of *substances*.

Empiricism
The belief that all knowledge of things outside the mind is acquired through sense experience.

Entail
In *logic*, when one thing inevitably follows from another.

Epistemology
The branch of philosophy concerned with what knowledge is, what we can know, and how we can know what we know.

Essence
The true nature of something— what makes it what it is.

Ethics
The study of right and wrong behavior and the moral principles that govern that behavior. Also known as *moral philosophy*.

Existentialism
An approach in 20th-century philosophy that focuses on human existence and the search for meaning or purpose in life.

Fallacy
An error of *reasoning* that is easily made.

Falsifiability
A statement, or set of statements, is said to be falsifiable if it can be shown to be false.

Fuzzy logic
A system of *logic* that deals with *half-truths*, allowing them to be expressed on a continuum between true and false.

Half-truth
A claim that is partially true.

Harm principle
Proposed by John Stuart Mill, the idea that people should be free to do what they want, provided this does not harm others, or restrict their freedom to do the same.

Hypothesis
A proposed explanation that is to be investigated further.

Idealism
The view that reality consists ultimately of minds and their ideas, rather than material things. The opposite view is *materialism*.

Induction
Inferring a *conclusion* from one or more *premises;* the *conclusion* is supposed to be supported but not logically *entailed* by the *premises*.

Inference
A *conclusion* drawn by means of an *argument* from *premises*.

Liberalism
In *political philosophy*, the view that society should protect individual freedom and equality.

Logic
The branch of philosophy that studies *rational argument*—including how to construct a good *argument* and identify flaws in *arguments*.

Logical form
In *logic*, the structure of an *argument*.

Materialism
The idea that ultimately everything is material. There are no nonmaterial *substances* or properties. The opposite view is *idealism*.

Metaphysics
The branch of philosophy concerned with the fundamental nature of reality.

Mind-body dualism
The view that mind and body are two separate *substances*.

Monism
The view that there is ultimately just one *substance*.

Moral philosophy
Also known as *ethics*, the branch of philosophy that examines ideas of right and wrong, good and bad, and the moral basis for our actions and judgments.

Morality
Principles that determine right and wrong, or good and bad behavior.

Necessary truth
Something that must be the case— the opposite of a *contingent truth*.

Noumenon
A *thing-in-itself*, which exists independently of our experience, beyond the scope of our minds— the opposite of *phenomenon*.

Paradox
An *argument*, which, despite apparently sound *reasoning* from acceptable *premises*, leads to a *conclusion* that seems absurd.

Phenomenon
Something that we can experience. This is the opposite of *noumenon*.

Philosophy of mind
The branch of philosophy that studies the nature of the mind, mental processes, consciousness, and the relationship of the mind to the physical body.

Physicalism
The belief that ultimately everything is physical. For example, our mental experiences can be explained through the physical workings of our brains.

Pineal gland
A tiny gland in the brain that looks like a pine cone. René Descartes believed this to be the point where the mind connects to the body.

Political philosophy
The branch of philosophy that examines the nature and methods of the state, including the concepts of justice, politics, and social order.

Pragmatism
A philosophical approach that emphasizes the usefulness of knowledge—a theory or belief is successful if it can be practically applied.

Premise
The starting point of an *argument*. Any *argument* must start from at least one premise—for example, "All men are mortal."

Primary and secondary qualities
In the philosophy of John Locke, an object has primary qualities, which can be measured independently of experience—such as size—and secondary qualities, which are determined by personal experience of that object—such as color.

Proof
An *argument* that establishes the truth of its *conclusion* beyond doubt.

Property dualism
The notion that physical things have nonphysical properties, such as mental properties.

Proposition
What is asserted when one makes a claim. Propositions can be true or false.

Rational
Based on, or at least not contrary to, the principles and use of *logic* and reason.

Rationalism
The belief that all knowledge is acquired through *rational* thought, or *reasoning*. The opposite view is known as *empiricism*.

Reasoning
Thinking about something in a logical, *rational* way.

Relativism
The notion that what is true or false depends upon cultural, social, or historial context.

Skepticism
The view that we do not or cannot have knowledge in a particular area. For example, skeptics about the external *world* say that we cannot know about the *world* outside our own minds.

Social contract
When members of a society implicitly agree to cooperate in order to achieve goals that benefit the group as a whole, sometimes at the expense of individuals within it.

Soul
The spiritual, immaterial part of a being, which is supposed to live on after death.

Substance
Something that is capable of existing on its own. For example, a mental substance could exist on its own, without any physical substance. Materialists say there is just one kind of substance— material substance. Dualists claim there are two kinds of substances: mental and physical.

Syllogism
A form of *reasoning* in which a *conclusion* is drawn from two *premises*. An example of a syllogism is "All men are mortal. Socrates is a man. Therefore, Socrates is mortal."

Synthetic proposition
A *proposition* that is not true by virtue of the meanings of the words used to express it. The opposite is an *analytic proposition*.

Thing-in-itself
What a thing actually is, rather than what it is as perceived through our senses. Another term for *noumenon*.

Thought experiment
An imaginary situation that is conceived for the purpose of testing a *hypothesis*.

Truth of fact
A true statement that cannot be established by reason alone (unlike a *truth of reasoning*).

Truth of reasoning
A statement that can be established as true through reason alone—unlike a *truth of fact*.

Utilitarianism
A theory in *moral* and *political philosophy* that judges the *morality* of an action by its consequences, and regards the most desirable outcome as the greatest good for the greatest number of people.

Validity
An *argument* is said to be valid if its *conclusion* follows logically from its *premises*. This does not mean that the *conclusion* is true.

Verifiability
A statement can be verified if it can be shown to be true.

World
In philosophy, the words *world*, *universe*, and *cosmos* are often used to mean the whole of reality that we can experience. Philosophers also sometimes refer to different "worlds," such as the *phenomenal* world, or the *noumenal* world.

World of ideas (or forms)
According to Plato, a *world*, separate from the *world* we live in, that contains ideal forms of things. We only ever see imperfect reflections of these perfect forms.

Zombie
In philosophy, a person who looks and behaves like a normal human, but who has no consciousness.

Index

Acknowledgments

DK would like to thank John Searcy for proofreading, and Jackie Brind for the index.

The publisher would like to thank the following for their kind permission to reproduce their photographs:

(Key: a–above; b–below/bottom; c–center; f–far; l–left; r–right; t–top)

6 Corbis: Lawrence Manning (fcr). **Fotolia:** dundanim (cl). **iStockphoto.com:** traveler1116 (fcl). **7 Getty Images:** Image Source (cl/scientist). **iStockphoto.com:** urbancow (cr). **10 Alamy Images:** Blend Images. **13 Dorling Kindersley:** Rough Guides / Brice Minnigh (br). **15 Corbis:** George Tatge / Alinari Archives (tr). **17 Corbis:** Richard T. Nowitz (br). **19 Dorling Kindersley:** Sir John Soane's Museum, London (br). **21 Corbis:** Stephen Simpson (br). **25 Dreamstime.com:** Eric Isselee (br/lion, br/tiger). **33 Corbis:** Hyungwon Kang / Reuters (br). **35 Dorling Kindersley:** Rough Guides / Roger Norum (cra). **38 Corbis:** Halfdark / fstop. **40 Science Photo Library:** Laguna Design (bl). **42 Fotolia:** Paul Paladin (bl). **47 Dorling Kindersley:** Birmingham Buddhist Vihara (br). **51 Alamy Images:** AF archive (br). **64–65 Alamy Images:** Henry Arden / Cultura Creative (RF). **67 Fotolia:** Valdis Torms (br). **79 Alamy Images:** Photos 12 (br). **88 Alamy Images:** Image Source / IS026617R. **95 Dorling Kindersley:** Science Museum, London (bc). **99 Wikipedia:** (tr). **101 Alamy Images:** Hugh Threlfall (tr). **104 Pearson Asset Library:** Pearson Education Ltd / Jules Selmes (b). **106–107 Getty Images:** Hulton Archive / Dorling Kindersley (artwork). **111 Alamy Images:** Brian Hagiwara / Brand X Pictures (br). **116 Alamy Images:** YAY Media AS / BDS. **118: Dorling Kindersley:** Whipple Museum of History of Science, Cambridge (bl). **122–123 Getty Images:** G. Dagli Orti / De Agostini / Dorling Kindersley (artwork). **132 Corbis:** Alfredo Dagli Orti / The Art Archive (bl). **137 Alamy Images:** Everett Collection Historical (br). **Dorling Kindersley:** Corbis / Hulton-Deutsch Collection. **141 Corbis:** Leonard de Selva (br). **143 Corbis:** Chris Hellier (tr). **144 Dorling Kindersley:** Rough Guides / Lydia Evans (b).

All other images © Dorling Kindersley
For further information see: www.dkimages.com